ANTON WEBERN

ANTON WEBERN

FRIEDRICH WILDGANS

*Translated by Edith Temple Roberts
and Humphrey Searle*

*With an Introduction and notes by
Humphrey Searle*

NEW YORK
OCTOBER HOUSE INC

FIRST PUBLISHED IN THE UNITED STATES 1967

BY OCTOBER HOUSE INC / NEW YORK
LIBRARY OF CONGRESS CATALOGUE NO. 67-26319
© CALDER AND BOYARS LIMITED, LONDON, 1966

PRINTED IN GERMANY

CONTENTS

TRANSLATOR'S PREFACE

Since his tragic death in 1945 Anton Webern has become probably the most discussed composer of modern times, and his influence on the younger generation of composers has been enormous. Yet little has been written about his life, and Professor Wildgans' book appears to be the first full biography. It may help to dispel many illusions about Webern's character and attitude to composition: for instance, the complicated mathematical analyses of his works published in Die Reihe Vol. 2 (Universal Edition) by Henri Pousseur, Karlheinz Stockhausen, Armin Klammer and others would have left Webern speechless, especially as (as Professor Wildgans now reveals) when at school he lacked all interest in mathematics and was extremely bad at this subject: his interests lay in the field of literature and the classics.

Professor Friedrich Wildgans was born in Vienna in 1913, and died a few months before the publication of his book. He studied composition with Joseph Marx and clarinet with Victor Polatschek. He was a professor at the Mozarteum in Salzburg from 1934–6, and then became a principal clarinettist of the Vienna State Opera Orchestra. From 1938–1945 he was persecuted by the Nazis because of his political beliefs, but in 1945 he was appointed Professor at the Vienna Academy, and he later became President of the Austrian Section of the International Society for Contemporary Music. Apart from his virtuosity as a clarinet player he was well known as a composer. His wife, Ilona Steingruber, is also well known as an interpreter of contemporary music – one of her most famous roles is Berg's "Lulu".

As a small personal tribute from one who was lucky enough to have had the chance of studying with Webern, I would like to reprint here an article which I wrote for the "Sunday Telegraph" in April 1961, as part of their series "Music's great teachers as seen by their pupils": it is republished by kind permission of the Editor. I had not read Professor Wildgans' book when I wrote the article, but I was glad to find that my estimate of Webern's character and artistic position corresponds well with that of one who knew him very much longer than I did.

"I came to study with Webern in a somewhat unusual way. When I was 19 I heard the first English performance of 'Wozzeck,' broadcast in 1934 under Sir Adrian Boult, and though I knew practically nothing about atonal music I was so moved and impressed by this that I determined to find out more.

"It so happened that Dr. Theodor Wiesengrund-Adorno, a pupil of Schoenberg and Webern and a leading exponent of Schoenbergian principles, had come to Oxford at that time as a refugee from Hitler's Germany, and when, a few years later, I was awarded the Octavia Travelling Scholarship from the Royal College of Music, he strongly advised me to go to Vienna and study with Webern, and even persuaded Sir Hugh Allen, then Director of the R.C.M., to agree to this.

"So, early in September 1937, I arrived in Vienna and at once went to see Webern. He was living in a village called Maria Enzersdorf, near Mödling, about 12 miles south of Vienna, and his house was on the outskirts of the village, almost in the woods. His circumstances were modest, and he and his family had only the upper half of a small two-storey house.

"He asked what I had done: I showed him some student compositions and explained that at Oxford I had read classics and philosophy and had only been allowed to study music as a side-line. So we decided to study Schoenberg's 'Harmonielehre' from the beginning, and during the next six months he took me through that remarkable book step by step, illuminating the text for me in an uncanny way as we went on.

"What might appear coldly theoretical in print he transformed into living music; for instance, when I wrote exercises based on the examples in Schoenberg's book he invariably played them over on the piano, and he was as much interested in the actual sound of them as in their theoretical construction. At my first lesson he talked absorbingly for an hour simply on the properties of the chord of C major; to him the laws of music were a living evolutionary process, not a set of abstract formulae laid down by theorists.

"This idea of evolution was very important to him and was the basis of his view of life and art; a fanatical lover of Nature, he felt in the same way that music had developed along a logical evolutionary path which led from the Middle Ages through the works of the great classical and romantic composers to the twelve-note method. That is to say, he did not regard the music of Schoenberg and his followers as providing a contrast to that of the past, but rather as a logical extension of it.

In fact, he had a great admiration for some of the romantic composers with whom one would have thought he had little in common. I had gone through a period of adulation of Wagner in my schooldays, but by this time was undergoing the inevitable reaction against him: but when I ventured to criticise Wagner Webern soundly berated me. 'Wagner was a great composer', he said 'and you cannot possibly say that you do not like him.'

"Similarly he greatly admired Bruckner, and we sometimes played his symphonies together as piano duets, Webern remarking on one occasion in the slow movements of the 7th symphony, 'Could your Elgar write an arch of melody like that?'.

"After we had finished our study of the 'Harmonielehre', Webern analysed for me various twelve-note works, including his own recently completed Piano Variations. He was prepared to do this for me as a composition student; but he felt that audiences and even performers did not need to know the technical processes by which twelve-note music is constructed.

"His approach was always practical rather than theoretical: he invariably used the piano while composing, trusting to his extraordinarily acute ear as well as to his

knowledge of the laws of music. On this point he said
to me once, 'Don't trust your ears alone; your ears will
always guide you aright, but you must also know what
you are doing.' These twin principles of knowledge
and practice were, I believe, the basis of his approach
to music.

"Webern led a very secluded life at this time; his
Workers' Chorus and Orchestra, which he had trained
and conducted with astonishing success, had been dis-
banded by the Dollfuss Government, and apart from his
teaching, his principal outside activity was the series of
private lectures in which he analysed works of composers
from Bach to Schoenberg with extraordinary acuteness.

"He was a simple man in many ways; as a convinced
social democrat he was in opposition to the right-wing
government of Schuschnigg and even believed that he
might fare better under the Nazis, who at least called
themselves socialists. In this he was cruelly disappointed
after the Anschluss, for the Nazis even forbade his private
teaching, and he had eventually to earn his living as a
proof-reader at his own publishers.

"Even before the Anschluss his music was only played
in Vienna at the chamber concerts given by the Austrian
section of the I.S.C.M., and it was little performed outside Austria; he would certainly have been astonished at
his present world-wide fame.

"Nevertheless, such considerations did not greatly matter to him; he simply knew that he was doing what was
right, and whether other people accepted this or not was
not of great importance to him. He was indeed an idealist

but one who remained very conscious of the world around him; he certainly did not shut himself up in an ivory tower.

"I left Vienna at the end for February, 1938, shortly before the Anschluss: I had hoped to return to study with him in the following winter, but this proved impossible, and we never met again, though we remained in correspondence up to the outbreak of the war.

"The 1938 I.S.C.M. Festival in London really began his international fame with the first performance of 'Das Augenlicht' under Scherchen, and in the following year I was able to conduct the first public performance in England of his Five Movements (Op. 5) in their string orchestral version, a performance in which he took a great interest.

"Now at last his genius is universally recognised; and I for one will always be grateful to him for his guidance and his example."

H. S.

AUTHOR'S PREFACE

THIS SMALL BOOK is the first to attempt a general description of the life and work of the Austrian composer, Anton
Webern. Conscious of the fact that within its limitations many facts will have to be omitted and many letters
and documents cannot be mentioned, the author nevertheless hopes that the main purpose of his book has not
been entirely missed. This is to present Anton Webern,
who is so much mentioned and argued about nowadays
by the younger generation of composers, as his acquaintances, his friends, pupils and colleagues knew him, and
thus provide an opportunity of correcting various mis-
conceptions, which Webern, the full-blooded musician,
constantly encounters among the younger generation
who consider themselves able to "continue his artistic
path".

Webern was always a musician, inspired by his muse,
musicality and feelings, and not by sterile intellectual
speculations. If he did pursue these, then the conclusions
he drew from them simply served to justify his theoretical concepts.

Only those who appreciated Webern as a man and a
musician in this way can claim a real understanding of

his music – certainly not from the point of view of serial speculation, which tends to be the order of the day nowadays when people discuss Webern and his music.

In meeting the publishers' request to tell the story of Webern's life and work, I have been helped by many people and institutions, who I should like to thank here. First of all Webern's daughters, Amalia Waller and Maria Halbich, who readily allowed me to inspect Webern's diaries and sketch-books; Mrs. Helene Berg (Alban Berg's widow), and Professor Dr. Ernst Diez, who lent me some most valuable letters of Webern; Webern's publishers in Vienna, the Universal Edition, who provided me with the more important data of Webern's creative activity and development; and finally Webern's friend and colleague from his period of study with Schoenberg, Dr. Josef Polnauer, who gave me much valuable insight into Webern and his life. Much material has also been taken from previous publications on Webern and his work, none of them exhaustive. Here I should like especially to mention Dr. Polnauer's valuable publication of the correspondence between Webern and his friend Hildegard Jone, the author of many of his texts, and Dr. Willi Reich's publication of Webern's two series of lectures "Paths to New Music" and "The Path to 12-Note Music", which includes a selection of Webern's letters in his possession from the dark years between 1934 and 1944; this also provided me with most valuable biographical material.

In the appendix dealing with Webern's works (as in the rest of the book), wherever possible I have allowed

Webern to speak for himself. It seemed to me that the
attitude of the composer to his works would appear more
important, more to the point and more interesting than
any attempt at interpretation by an outside observer at a
later date. In the same way I believed that the best way
to reproduce the substance of Webern's sensitive lyrical
temperament would be to publish some poems of his early
youth from about 1901; and also to add the glowing profession of faith of the Schoenberg pupil in his master in
the original form of 1912. Some excerpts from contemporary speeches and essays about Webern complete
the appendix.

Clearly within the confines of this short book it is barely possible to do full justice to the gifts and importance
and last but not least, to the sympathetic, sane humanity
of Anton Webern. Nevertheless, the author has considered it his prime duty to do the best within his abilities
in the hope of carrying the reader with him.

FRIEDRICH WILDGANS
Formerly Professor at the Academy of Music
and Dramatic Art, Vienna

ANTON WEBERN

To look at the life of the Austrian musician Anton von Webern is to be struck by the lack of anything outstandingly sensational about it. From the outside it appeared throughout an average, almost *petit bourgeois* existence; and what was generally known and accepted about the composer added little to change this concept. To those who knew him slightly Webern always appeared a spiritually simple man (he was never sociable or in need of the company of others), who used his musical talent and his ability to compose as a "gift from higher powers", but who generally was careful not to say or reflect too much on it or to put his art – or his interpretation of others' music – on a purely intellectual level. His spiritual interests were indeed one-sided; his literary taste was simple and almost naive and far removed from the ideal of a many-sided and deep culture that might have been expected from an artist of Webern's calibre and rank. Until late in life, for example, Webern had difficulties with the niceties of spelling, which sometimes led to almost grotesque results, as some of his letters show. Nevertheless, from his schooldays on he retained a warm interest in the classics, even if this touched the border of simplicity.

On the other hand, he lacked all interest in mathematics and in general school subjects, for which he also rarely obtained good marks during his secondary school education. He matriculated as a result of general goodwill towards him. (It is important to state this here, since when remembered it would seem absurd to hold Webern responsible for having founded the so-called "serial" technique of the young composers to-day. It would completely exclude the inspired, sensitive moment of "musical creation" in favour of intellectual construction and precise disciplines of calculation and measurement. This is exactly the sphere in which Webern never felt at home (that is, never since his earliest school days)).

It was a world with which he, a sensitive, instinctively musical man could never be satisfied. Webern was always an enthusiastic naturalist, fond of walking, of mountaineering, an amateur botanist, and above all a devoted, utterly faithful father – the representative of a legendary ideal that today barely survives – the classical "bonus pater familias". This ideal, nevertheless, may show traces of the *petit bourgeois* in our circles, a danger which even Webern could not completely escape. Superficially, he seemed to lack the spiritual breadth, generosity and adaptibility of the born artist; he certainly did not make his life easy and he suffered more than the average person from material conditions. That he should have developed thus may, to a large extent, have been due to his parentage, an influence which he was never quite able to overcome, even if, during the years of maturity, the ideals of his parents were no longer completely his own.

Anton Webern's father was a mining engineer, an offical of the former Royal Austrian Ministry of Agriculture who rose to the rank of Departmental Head, i. e., to the highest Austrian official grade. He came from an old Austrian aristocratic family which had settled in Carinthia for centuries; their family castle was in Salurn in the South Tyrol, near Bozen, and their full name was "Weber Freiherr von Webern". Anton Webern's father, Carl von Webern (1850–1919), was the first of his family to drop the title of "Freiherr" for the simple "von". Later, after the end of the first world war, titles were abolished by law throughout Austria. Nevertheless, Anton Webern was repeatedly described as "von Webern" on posters and on concert programmes, though he never referred to himself thus.

From surviving testimonials, and also from the obituary in the Austrian technical mining journal, it becomes clear that Webern's father was an exceptional, highly regarded technician, who was repeatedly appointed to positions of honour and who several times was decorated with the highest orders. He was one of the founders of a technical college which today is internationally esteemed as the "Montanistische Hochschule" (Mining College) in Leoben (Styria); later because of his many achievements it gave him its honorary doctorate.

In 1877 Carl von Webern married Amalie Antonia Gehr, the daughter of a master butcher from Mürzzuschlag in Styria. Three children were born to them, Anton Friedrich Wilhelm, born on 3rd December 1883, being the second child and the only son. The home in which Webern grew up had a pleasant bourgeois, but not especially artistic atmosphere. His father, though he had no active artistic tendencies, was nevertheless an educated and well-read man; he created the spiritual framework in which Anton developed. Early on, at the age of five, his mother, a woman interested in the arts and a good amateur pianist, introduced him to music and to the piano. This early period of piano tuition, which in no way provided a clue to the musical gift he was to show, coincides with the period of his early childhood in Vienna, and then with his years at school in Graz (1890–1894), where his father was transferred as mining supervisor. From 1894 onwards, Anton attended the grammar school at Klagenfurt, and there he matriculated in July 1902. This Klagenfurt period is important, in studying Webern's artistic childhood and youth, since it contains the years of his first serious and regular musical instruction; the young schoolboy was taught from about 1895 to 1902 by the Klagenfurt musician, Dr. Edwin Komauer. Principally, Dr. Komauer taught the young Webern the piano and 'cello. The latter he played in his youth with some passion, taking part in the Klagenfurt amateur orchestra as a 'cellist; and as we shall see later, he even thought of earning his living as an orchestral 'cellist at one time. Apparently, his music lessons with Dr. Komauer also included the beginnings of musical theory. No one today is in a position to report precisely on the form or content of these lessons, yet it may be assumed that they did not go deep and did not include anything more than those disciplines now internationally known as "General Music Teaching". But

in addition – and this was to be the most important facet
of his lessons with Dr. Komauer – through his teacher the
young Webern became familiar with the most important
classical and modern works of musical literature (a welcome addition to his experiences as an orchestral 'cellist)
through piano scores for two or four hands. This was at
a time, during the first years of the 20th century, when
radio did not yet exist and gramophone records were still
in their infancy. Thus, in a provincial town such as
Klagenfurt, one had to rely on local concerts and one's
own musical activities – the best if not the only way of
getting to know musical literature. Through Dr. Komauer
(who was only a local Carinthian musician, but known
as a good technician) Webern first received a practical
artistic education in music. Webern himself, in his diaries
of the early period, frequently spoke gratefully of the
enrichment Dr. Komauer's lessons provided: he seems to
have fully acknowledged the musical authority of his
teacher.

Through this part of his education – the playing of
various works in piano versions – Webern first came
across Gustav Mahler's works; but of this more elsewhere. Of the purely theoretical disciplines, such as
harmony, form, etc., Webern probably learnt little within
the framework of these lessons. Thus, the young man
could not fall back on a definite discipline when, for the
first time, he felt the need to express himself artistically
by composing some songs of his own. So it happens that,
round about 1901 judging by the handwriting, but in any
case during his final period at school, a diary entry speaks

of "Vier Lieder op. 1", and also mentions the poets of these songs. It says *op. 1, 4 Lieder*

1.   *Early Spring, (Vorfrühling)* E flat major
       (F. Avenarius "Stimmen und Bilder")
2.   *Cloudy Night, (Wolkennacht)* D flat major
3.   *From far away, deeply, (Tief von fern)* E major
       (Richard Dehmel)
4.   *Longing, (Wehmut)* B flat major
       (F. Avenarius "Stimmen und Bilder")
       and added in pencil at a later date:
5.   *Devout, (Fromm)* E flat major (G. Falke)

These songs were never mentioned again, either in letters or in diary notes, and as, until recently, no manuscripts or even sketches were known, it was assumed that they never existed, but remained as projects or plans which the 17-year-old schoolboy was unable to complete. Webern himself supported this supposition in a letter to his closest friend of the period, and the confidant of his youth, his cousin Ernst Diez, who was a few years older. (Diez later became known as a sociologist and university professor). Webern wrote on December 8th, 1901, "only the composing does not make progress; unfortunately, I achieve nothing". The truth of this sentiment can hardly be questioned.*

In spite of possible doubts and reservations, the note remains of interest to us, since it permits a glimpse into

---

* The manuscripts of some of these songs were in fact discovered later, and are now in the Webern Archive of the Moldenhauer Collection at the University of Washington, Seattle, U.S.A.

that literary world which during the early period formed
and dominated Webern's artistic leanings. As with so
many young people of the period the names of Richard
Dehmel, F. Avenarius, and Gustav Falke predominate, a
fact that fully corresponds to the general literary
tendencies of the time. It indicates no independent or
original literary position. The attempts at poetry (some
manuscripts in Webern's own hand from his later school
period have been discovered) were in no way different.
The poems echoed a spiritual atmosphere which was
generally characteristic of the spiritual and artistic pro-
duction of the turn of the century. From it flowed the
early manifestations of literary creation of which Schnitz-
ler, Hofmannsthal, Hauptmann and later Altenberg and
Schönherr were typical German representatives. This
literary world was to be the background of Webern's
early spiritual and artistic development.

Definite clues that help to reconstruct Webern's early
period are contained in two kinds of documents, since few
witnesses of the time remain. Firstly, there are Webern's
letters from the early period of his artistic development;
and secondly his earliest surviving musical works, which
mostly date from 1903 onwards.

The recipient of the letters which were to prove the
most valuable illumination of Webern's youthful years
was, and remained Ernst Diez. We know that he was
not only Webern's first and most important confidant
from his early school years, but that the two cousins usually spent their summer holidays on the Webern family
estate, Preglhof near Bleiburg, in Carinthia. Diez shared

with Webern an enthusiasm for walking and was also a keen naturalist. The letters written by the young Webern to his friend are more open and descriptive, more searching than his diary notes. The young Webern confided in his cousin his worries about school, his first loves, and also the difficult question of his future profession. Although a loving, grateful and respectful son, on this point Webern did not see eye to eye with his father. Webern's father wished above all to secure a living for his son, without the necessity of hard or menial work. As the elder sister had already married, and the younger was still under marriageable age, the father concentrated on his only son, who was not, however, pleased with this intensity of authoritarian parental concern about his career. A letter to Diez illuminates these difficulties and permits a glimpse into the differences separating father and son. Father Webern was in no way convinced of his son's musical gifts; in his view his son had shown too little talent to follow a musical career.

Anton, on the other hand, indulged in truly unreal and immature dreams about his future; clearly, he had no precise conception of how to realise it.

Thus, on 22nd July, 1901, he wrote to Diez, who was then a philosophy student in Graz: "And now a request. You know that I am doubtful and uncertain about where to turn regarding my future career. Perhaps you could discover something about the so-called *Hochschule für Musik* in Berlin, or the *Akademie der Tonkunst* in Munich. What one learns there, who attends, etc. The purely theoretical, scientific study of music naturally in-

terests me very much too, but ideally I should like a practical job, particularly as a conductor. Probably it will be
necessary to attend a Conservatorium to learn an instrument, for example, the 'cello for me, up to a master's
degree or at least to an advanced level, and then to join
an orchestra. If one is successful then one becomes a conductor. At least that is how I imagine it. Nikisch, for
example, has done it this way. Naturally, I should like
to embark at once on such a career, but father has his
doubts about my talent to the point where I begin to
doubt myself. Of course, I think of orchestras only in
terms of the large ones – concert or opera orchestras –
in Dresden, Leipzig, Munich, Berlin and other large
towns in Germany. But then I should be unable to look
after the running of Preglhof. I don't know at all what
to do with it. Let it? Sell it? Father's wish is that I should
study at the technical college of agriculture and then live
at Preglhof. Oh my God! And Art? Which means everything to me and for which I should like to make every
sacrifice? . . ."

Naturally, Webern's father wished to secure the future
of his much loved son in spite of several difficulties. To
his careful, unimaginative official mind it appeared to be
the most comfortable and least dangerous career to take
charge of the family estate and its agricultural lands and
to reap from them the greatest possible profit. There
would be sufficient free time for his son to play music,
compose and so on. The scant self-confidence of the
young man, evident from his letter, appeared to re-
inforce the reservations of the father. A few weeks before

this letter was sent Webern had passed his final examination at the Klagenfurt grammar school with generally average success, or at any rate with fairly high marks in the literary subjects and less good marks in the scientific subjects. It seemed he was better equipped for a career on the arts side. His father – perhaps happy that his son had passed his examination – promised him, and made possible a journey to Bayreuth for the Wagner Festival, a proof of his unprejudiced attitude which sought a real understanding with his son.

Thus Anton, accompanied by Ernst Diez, went to Bayreuth and there wrote more or less as his first serious attempt at literature, an exact discription of this "Pilgrimage to Bayreuth". In it we recognise the earliest signs of Anton Webern's artistic attitudes, a fiery, passionate, ecstatic attitude towards Richard Wagner and his "music drama". Then, after Anton's return from Bayreuth, father and son agreed that Anton should study music at the University of Vienna and should complete his studies with a doctorate in philosophy. Nothing more was said at the time, but the possibility of further discussion was not excluded. This decision was at least partially due to the fact that Webern's father, who had until then presided as Oberbergrat at the Klagenfurt Mining authority, was now called to Vienna to occupy the post of Ministerialrat at his Ministry there. So the whole household left Klagenfurt to settle in Vienna. With this move one problem that seemed to threaten the family, namely to allow Anton to go to Vienna by himself, was solved. The family left Klagenfurt, moved to Vienna, and soon settled in the Ferstgasse, behind the so-called "Votivkirche", in the ninth district. It was only a short way from the new apartment to the University, the place which until further notice – it was the autumn of 1902 – was to take charge of Anton's technical and artistic development. Here he was in luck. Guido Adler*, then professor of Music, carefully looked after all his pupils, especially the young Webern. He engaged as lecturers in his institute two well known music teachers, who at the time were much appreciated: Professor Hermann Graedener and Dr. Karl Navratil (both still known as theoreticians and practising composers). Those especially gifted in musicology, harmony, counterpoint and form came under the care of these two men. Graedener and Navratil, therefore, became the teachers whom the young Webern had to thank for his first real introduction into the disciplines of musical theory and practical composition. This was especially important, as the lessons in theoretical subjects with his otherwise excellent first music teacher in Klagenfurt, Dr. Edwin Komauer, had been rather superficial, and so had not provided Webern with any foundations for composition. Probably his inability to master the disciplines of classical composition was the real reason for his inability in Klagenfurt to attempt serious composing. Some attempts at composition do, however, survive from the years 1902 and 1903. They show the young Webern not only closely linked to the "Jugendstil" lyricism of the time,

* Guido Adler, 1855–1941, Austrian critic and historian. He edited the Handbuch der Musikgeschichte.

but musically demonstrate a close connection with the
post-romantic period (something like the style of the
young Richard Strauss and others), though somewhat
mixed with juvenile components, and revealing a certain
immaturity. Among the earliest surviving compositions
from Webern's hand are some sketches of Lieder, of
which "Aufblick", to a poem by Richard Dehmel, is the
most worked out. It is a harmless, somewhat clumsy song,
without precise thematic development and sorrowfully
romantic. It provides no inkling of Webern's later creative style, apart from an embryonic liking to take the
dynamic markings down to a threefold pianissimo and
to use a somewhat tearful chromaticism. This seems to
have had its origins in the post Wagnerian world, and
appears here clearly and unconcealed: later it was to
remain a basis of Webern's style, though varied by
changing the octave pitch of the intervals within the
melodic line, or concealed by a constant change of tone
colour within the melodic phrase (melody of tone colour)!
These are specific and characteristic components of
Webern's later musical language. A closer comparison
would almost certainly discover other points of departure
of his later, more mature musical expression.

Among the earliest sketched-out works that survive is
a Ballad on a text by Uhland – "Siegfried's Sword" for
baritone solo and orchestra. Because on one hand the
melody used here is quite unknown, and on the other, since
the substance of the ballad is totally foreign to the young
Webern's means of expression, it may be assumed that
this is no original composition, but an attempt to

orchestrate a melody popular at the time, an attempt moreover which was not completed, and which in its surviving fragments demonstrates little ability or imagination in the use of instrumental sound. But the manuscript, in ink, and dated "Preglhof, Summer 1930", undoubtedly shows the writing of the young Webern, even if the material, taken from the German heroic saga in the poetic, somewhat rhetorical form given it by Uhland, was quite foreign to his mentality. The effects of the intensively felt heroic Wagnerian atmosphere of Bayreuth may have influenced Webern, whose personal style had not yet developed. But it is neither inspired, nor, in its almost childish working–out is it even a successful echo of Wagner. For Webern's development the work is of no importance, and could be forgotten without loss. No similar attempts survive. It is only mentioned here for the sake of completeness among Webern's few surviving early works.

It may be assumed that the summer holidays spent at Preglhof were mainly reserved for composition (several of the early manuscripts carry both date and place), while term time was occupied more with the serious study of musicology. The atmosphere of Viennese music teaching in 1902, and the effects it was to have on the young Webern is clearly described in his letter to Diez of 5th November, 1902:

". . . I attend regular lectures in musical history. I am inscribed for three of Adler's lectures: 1) 'Periods of Musical Style'; 2) Explanations and Evaluations of Musical Works (at this moment: Mozart); 3) Exercises at the

Institute of Musical History. No. 2 consists of the students
doing talks about Mozart's works, from the smallest and
least significant to his greatest works. No. 3 is rather difficult: the Institute is attended mainly by older people,
two doctors, and other more advanced students. There
are three freshmen. The older ones give lectures about
theoreticians of the 13th, 14th and 15th centuries. They
are given parts of their works to translate and then
have to explain them. We young ones keep up as best
we can. For the time being my task is to absorb into
my brain as quickly as possible mensural notation and
a work by Riemann about this old music. A terribly dry
and laborious task: you have no idea how many rules there
are. The members of the Institute are: 7 Jews, one Jewess,
4 Poles and 4 Germans. When I went to the Institute for
the first time, I shuddered at the many difficulties; I
should have liked to have run away; the Jews were so
unfriendly, etc. Now I have got used to it. We have a
considerable music library, though oddly enough no
'Tannhäuser', 'Lohengrin', 'Meistersinger' or 'Parsifal',
and a magnificent Bösendorfer grand piano for use. I
spend almost all day at the Institute. I am also attending
lectures given by Dr. Wallaschek, who speaks about the
'Beginnings of Music', and by Dr. Müller about 'Practical Philosophy' – a fine chap who talks more about literature than philosophy. I do not attend Diez, since his
classes clash with Adler's, and in addition he is said to
have some defect of speech and to be 'anti-Wagnerian'. I
take harmony at the University with Professor Graedener,
counterpoint with a certain Dr. Navratil, whom Adler

has invited to the Institute for his pupils". This letter
gives a far more detailed glimpse of the University
atmosphere surrounding Webern than does his diary. It
also demonstrates certain critical social attitudes which
should not be misunderstood in any aggressive anti-
semitic sense. Webern's thoughts never ran to politics,
were never aggressively anti-semitic or "racialist", either
in his early days or in the darkest years of Austria
and Germany between 1933 and 1945. Webern's
lifelong admiration, or close personal friendship with
Jewish people – Mahler and Schoenberg, for example –
his spiritual tolerance and good nature, and his often
stressed friendly feelings for Jewish colleagues and pupils
would render such suspicions groundless. This needs to
be said since he was accused more than once of
sympathising with the philosophy of national-socialism.
But more about Webern's thoughts and reactions to political developments later.

Never, during the whole of his life, did Webern allow
his objective judgement in artistic matters to be clouded
by political, religious or racial sentiments. That the young
man, the son of a loving family, should somehow have
faced the demands of everyday life with difficulty, that
he, the music student, found it difficult to meet his colleagues on common ground – who does not comprehend
his problems? The need to fit into the University circle
may, in fact, have presented difficulties to the young
composer, at least at first. The letter cited above was
clearly written as a result of these first impressions.

Unfortunately few well authenticated reports of the

Vienna University years remain. Thus it is difficult to
reconstruct this important period of Webern's life with
any degree of thoroughness or detail. Apparently, Ernst
Diez was the only person in whom Webern fully confided during his youth, to whom he reported now and
again on his studies and their progress. It should be
remembered that his parents lived in the immediate
vicinity. By far the greater part of the letters to Diez –
which could have provided us with a deeper insight –
were devoted to reports about visits to opera and concerts. Nothing was more natural than that the young
music student, emerging from the isolation of the Austrian provinces, should immerse himself in the musical
atmosphere of the famous "City of Music". He went to
a large number of concerts and allowed many divergent
musical influences to overwhelm him.

At the time – the autumn and winter of 1902–03 –
everything could be seen and heard in Vienna: there
was too much even for Webern, who possessed an almost
boundless spiritual appetite. As he put it in his diary in
November 1903:

". . . Now the high tide of the concert season flows
with fearful strength. Too much! Too much! Every day
there are at least three concerts. Violin virtuosi, piano
virtuosi, male singers, female singers, orchestral concerts, etc. Every concert filled with people who applaud after every item. Whether it is good or bad, they
do not care. Perhaps – no, certainly – the people can no
longer tell the difference. As a result of too much, their
attention, their ability to enjoy, is increasingly lessened,

and as a result of the poor programmes and the 'magic
arts' of the virtuosi their taste is spoilt for good. There
is no ruthless criticism ... Supposing it goes on? ..."

Alongside the artistic impressions offered by the city
went a desire by the young musician to participate ac-
tively in these events. Having been used to playing the 'cello
in the Klagenfurt amateur orchestra, he took part in different amateur choral societies as chorus repetiteur. He
also tried his hand, as was common at the time, as a chamber musician in amateur music circles. These were all
activities which, in furthering his musical education and
experience and enriching his knowledge of literature,
should not be underestimated. First he joined the "Aka-
demische Wagner-Verein" as an active member and sang
in its chorus. Here he hoped to find new nourishment for
his deep admiration for the master of Bayreuth, and to
make connections with the well-known musicians of the
time – a hope that was to be only partially fulfilled. At
the Wagner-Verein, Webern met several famous conductors of the period (among them Felix Mottl, Hans
Richter, Arthur Nikisch, and not least Gustav Mahler);
with some of them he achieved a more personal, if temporary, contact, as for example with Gustav Mahler. In
spite of Webern's earlier sharp criticism of Mahler, he
learnt to admire him greatly, to become in later years one
of the most enthusiastic, most feeling and stylistically
most sure interpreters of his music. As a member of the
chorus he was able to take part in several great performances of classical and modern works which filled him
with special satisfaction.

Only in Vienna did Webern realise what the all-round
musical instruction of his teacher in Klagenfurt, Dr.
Edwin Komauer, had meant, even though he was aware
that he owed his introduction into the secrets of harmony,
counterpoint and practical composition to the two University teachers already mentioned, Dr. Navratil and Professor Graedener. Soon he sought to continue his 'cello
lessons (with the then first 'cellist of the Vienna Concert-
Verein Orchestra) and the piano (with a young American
music student, a pupil of Leschetizky, whom Webern did
not mention by name in his letters: she also helped the
Webern family to buy a piano). But soon Webern gave
up the 'cello completely, and for the rest of his life he
remained a fairly poor piano player; he could read at
sight, but never again practised to improve his technique.
Never again did he need practical instrumental discipline: for his activities as a chorus repetiteur his technique
was sufficient.

Besides this there were his studies at the University.
Under Adler's guidance he acquired the necessary
knowledge for a student of musicology: mensural notation,
deciphering of neumes and the forms and laws of early
polyphony. But there was one drawback – in spite of the
fascinating substance of his musicological studies. For
Webern, with his constant desire for a creative musical
existence, the very general requirements in the study of
composition made by Drs. Navratil and Graedener, which
took little account of individual wishes, were too barren
and dry. Probably at the time he was thinking of more
ambitious creative plans. His desire to find a teacher who

was a composer in his own right steadily grew. It is certain
that none of the masters of composition living in Vienna
was his choice. Mahler, whom Webern admired and
whom he would have liked as his teacher, hardly taught
at all, probably because he was too busy as Director of
the Opera. It is impossible to ascertain today who it
was who mentioned the name of Hans Pfitzner to the
young Webern as a possible teacher in composition.
The fact is that Webern went to Berlin in the spring
of 1904, together with the young conductor, Dr. Heinrich Jalovec, who was later to be a co-pupil with
Webern of Schoenberg's, and whom Webern may have
met at the University. It was both Webern's and Jalovec'
intention to became Pfitzner's pupils in composition.
Since all personal evidence about their intention, its realisation and the success of their plan is lacking, nothing
definite can be said here. According to Dr. Polnauer, a
later fellow-student under Schoenberg and a friend of
Webern's, it seems that Webern's intention to take composition under Pfitzner in Berlin was impossible to realise. Apparently (this comes from another source) Pfitzner
was said to have let fall some slighting remarks about
Mahler when talking to Webern. Thereupon the young
man turned round and returned to Vienna. There he
explained that he neither could nor would study with
Pfitzner. So there was no further question of a move.

This period, when the decisions affecting Webern's
future as a composer were hanging in the air, must have
been an interesting one. Unfortunately, we know nothing
from Webern's own hand about it. Another decision

at the time might have made a great difference to
Webern's hitherto undeveloped style in composition and
expression.

There was, too, a pause in the letters to Diez; above
all Webern seems to have failed to report to his friend
about his Berlin experiences. His diary notes of the
time – 1904 – which were soon to cease altogether, remained silent. Whether Webern kept another diary which
has not survived is unknown, but it can hardly be assumed. What survives in the existing diaries is almost
completely limited to purely personal reflections of an
intimate kind, or else to personal experiences in the
theatre or at concerts, which add little to the general
picture.

After the failure of the excursion to Pfitzner, a suitable
teacher in composition in Vienna had now to be found.
Today it is no longer certain when and in what manner
and on whose recommendation Webern came into contact with Schoenberg and took lessons from him. According to some sources, Guido Adler sent some of his most
gifted and remarkable pupils to Schoenberg for lessons, i. e. those most adept at music and musicology from
whom he hoped for creative work. Schoenberg had
already acquired an excellent reputation in Vienna, if in
a limited circle, as an original and responsible teacher.
Clearly, in Adler's eyes Webern was one of these
promising young talents. Unfortunately, Webern does
not even mention his first meeting with Schoenberg
in his diaries; nor does he mention Adler's initiative in
putting him in touch with Schoenberg. Thus, it is impos-

sible to reconstruct the exact events that led to Webern's
meeting with Schoenberg. What is certain is that Webern
showed some works to Schoenberg about the middle of
1904; these must have been the attempts at Lieder already
mentioned. On this basis Schoenberg began to teach
Webern from the autumn of 1904 onwards.

Webern did not note down anything about the manner
of his lessons which has survived. This is surprising, since
Schoenberg's teaching methods were radically different
from those prevailing at the time at any official institute,
or even privately. Later – in 1912 – in his essay "Schoenberg, the Teacher", Webern wrote at length on this theme.
Looking back, perhaps subjectively, he spoke of the manner of Schoenberg's teaching, his ethical and spiritual
position in his composition classes, all of it in an understanding and convincing manner. The extent to which
these lessons enriched the young Webern becomes clear
from this, lessons taken with a completely unconventional
and highly original fiery spirit – as we must regard the
Schoenberg of that period – even though he may not
always have been "agreeable". These lessons went well
beyond purely artistic matters to the spiritual and philosophical, forming and educating the pupil. It was given
to Schoenberg with his sure diagnostic touch to recognise
in each young composer what rudimentary or embryonic
musical gifts existed, and that without regard for any
particular direction of style. Above all, he recognised the
degree of potential creative personality, which he developed by suitable means of artistic education in each of
his pupils to the point where the existing talents of a

truly creative personality were brought to their highest
point in every respect.

This was exactly the right kind of teacher from whom
the young Webern, whose creative talents at this point
had remained undeveloped – he was "a blank page" as
it were – could learn a great deal; and this was so, even
if Schoenberg with his often dictatorial ways, and as a
result of his powerful personality and his masterly language, may at first have "flattened" Webern.

Schoenberg as a teacher – at least in his early aggressive days – probably acted in a way similar to the non-
commissioned officers of the armies of the old Austria
and Germany. They took it upon themselves first to
destroy the personality and then the self-confidence of
their recruits as thoroughly as possible, and to recreate
from the fragments of the old, broken personality a new
creature according to a different pattern. Schoenberg at the
beginning of his teaching career was naturally motivated
by a higher sense. It seemed essential to him, and in line
with his plan, first of all to destroy those traditions which
had been wrongly understood and to do away with false-
ly based aesthetic ideals. Only then did he graft a
new personality on to the spirit that had been rid of all
ballast. Schoenberg lived and thought for his pupils, but
he demanded that they should do likewise, that his pupils
should serve him, that they should dedicate to him and
present him with everything they could produce. Thus
Schoenberg – pointing to the educational value of such
measures – allowed his pupils to do lengthy and time-consuming corrections to his scores, to make piano versions

of them, or similar tasks. He allowed them to help him financially and with gifts of food; they presented him with valuable presents, and looked after the smaller and larger requirements of his everyday life, a fact shown clearly in the letters Schoenberg's pupils wrote to each other.

We may imagine Schoenberg the teacher as a rich, many-sided, animated personality, who could also be selfish, incredibly egotistical and egocentric. This fact, supplemented by Webern's later essay "Schoenberg, the Teacher", may give us an idea of the sort of impressions that flowed from Schoenberg's original mind to the youthful musician. And we shall be able to understand the position taken up by the young musicians: they could choose between admiration without reservation to the point of self-annihilation, or open opposition. At the time of which we speak there could be no question of this latter choice.

Among the Schoenberg pupils of these early years was Alban Berg, among others who were to play smaller parts in Webern's biography. Berg, the composer of "Wozzeck", was to become Webern's close friend; until his early death in 1935 they often corresponded – a fact which was to have an important bearing on Webern's later life. Through these letters to Berg – a colleague of somewhat similar personality – we learn of many intimate aspects of Webern's inner life, of his work, his surroundings, his circumstances, his attitudes to many things that happened to him and moved him. These letters contain indispensable material for the biographer since, after 1906,

Webern ceased to keep a diary for a lengthy period: and
the correspondence with the friend of his early youth,
Ernst Diez, became relatively unimportant, since both
lived in the same town (Vienna), and so preferred to ex-
change their thoughts in person rather than by letter.

But to return to Webern's period of study. Before
starting on his lessons with Schoenberg, his studies at the
University probably took first place in Webern's spiritual life, (that is, before the autumn of 1904). Once under
Schoenberg's spell there remained little room for other
things. At least in 1903, Webern was still energetically
pursuing his musicological studies, and also his lessons as
a 'cellist and pianist. In a letter sent to Diez on 18th
February, 1903, in Graz, where his cousin was an apprentice teacher in philosophy for a year, he wrote:

". . . my piano, 'cello and counterpoint studies flourish
and bear fruit. I have even done something for musical
science. To practise my knowledge in mensural notation
I transcribed a piece 'Sacris solemniis' by Brassart*. I do
not even know the century; but it's nice that it will be
published, namely in the 'Denkmäler der Tonkunst in
Oesterreich'. You can imagine my courage rising, since
it was not easy. But no, I am praising myself. Please forgive me, dear Ernst, but I am overjoyed with my activity".

Apart from these and similar extracts from the diaries
and letters already quoted, we know little about the
form or stages of Webern's university studies, which

---

* A Belgian contrapuntalist who lived in the 15th century as a
singer in the Papal choir in Rome.

ended in the summer of 1906 with his promotion to Doctor
of Philosophy. Webern's thesis, at the he request of Adler,
was on the old Flemish master who had been intimately
connected with Austria, Heinrich Ysaac. Webern later
used parts of his thesis in his edition of the second
volume of the works and life of Heinrich Ysaac in the
"Denkmäler der Tonkunst in Oesterreich".

Webern appears to have been satisfied with the external distinction of a doctor's degree. Probably he sought
to achieve this only to justify his choice of profession to
his father, who had helped him so generously in this
respect. He was never again to take up musicological
work. On the contrary, the text of his lecture series about
modern music (of which a shorthand transcript exists)
given before a private audience in Vienna in the thirties,
("Weg zur neuen Musik" and "Der Weg zur Musik mit
zwölf Tönen") ("Paths to modern music", and "The
Path to music with twelve notes") in its naïvity and
intentionally popular language shows little trace of his
previous musicological training.

Few details of the period from 1904 onwards when
Webern studied composition under Schoenberg are
known; and nothing at all about the first months of these
studies. Polnauer's reports deal only with the later stages.

The fact is that Webern's few surviving, so far unpub-
lished, compositions and attempts at composition, which
he wrote under Schoenberg's supervision during the four
years of study, present the best testimony of the intensity
and sensible planning of these lessons; they demonstrate
the pupil's considerable technical progress compared to

his pre-Schoenberg attempts. If the form of the pieces (Lieder) of the early period were incredibly naive, clumsy and wooden, the work done under Schoenberg's guidance already shows a more thorough, sensitive and architectonically comprehensible approach, built on the classics. These works were the Sonata movement for piano of 1905 and the early Lieder, of which some in modified form were later to be issued as op. 3.* When and where the individual Lieder of this cycle were composed can no longer be definitely ascertained, since Webern's papers show many gaps. But it cannot be doubted that they were conceived – at least the majority of them – during the period of study with Schoenberg. It seems probable, too, that the chorus "Entflieht auf leichten Kähnen" stems from sketches done during the period of study with Schoenberg.

A broadly worked piece in one movement, resembling sonata form, for the traditional piano quintet combination (2 violins, viola, 'cello and piano) can be definitely dated, according to Webern's colleagues, to 1907. Webern himself said next to nothing about this early work; the original manuscript is unfortunately not now available. One sees here the detailed working out of motivic and thematic connections, in the stressing of the idea of form and in the architectonic concept of the work. It is more concentrated and integral than the piano movement of 1905 (though this was carefully thought out): it shows the in-

* For details of further early works see Dr. Moldenhauer's Catalogue of the Webern Archive at the University of Washington, Seattle, 1964.

fluence of Schoenberg's early teaching, which laid stress
on the importance of connecting, particularly in the classical sense, through thematic and motivic relations and
the logical development of the basic musical elements.
From the piano movement of 1905 to the piano quintet
of 1907 a progressive firmness and definition in the use
of traditional methods of composition can be clearly
perceived. Josef Polnauer, at that time in constant touch
with Webern, reports that the latter was composed more
or less as a tribute to his mother, who had died at Preglhof in 1906.

Schoenberg, who accepted Webern's piano quintet as
a serious proof of his talent, had it played before an
invited audience at a private house in Vienna in 1907.
Since then the piece, which Webern dismissed as a youthful work, and did not provide with an opus number, was
not played again during Webern's lifetime. Possibly encouraged by Schoenberg's favourable judgment, Webern
may have thought of re-working it later on and publishing
it. But he did not realise the project; the work was
only published after Webern's death by an American
publisher, Bomart, in facsimile in 1946.

No other works that Schoenberg may have demanded
from his pupil during the period of study are known,
apart from the exercises written for his lessons.

Thus the "Passacaglia", later to be called "Opus 1" is
all the more intersting. It was the last work Webern completed more or less under Schoenberg's eyes. It was written with a great sense of responsibility, with love and
with a mature technique built on classical models. It

proved, in fact, that Webern in his lessons with Schoenberg had mastered the traditional means of composition. Webern himself repeatedly referred to his "Passacaglia" as ending his apprenticeship – a "Gesellenstück" – a concept which undoubtedly came from a remark of Schoenberg's. Naturally, Webern remained glad of Schoenberg's criticism, later on too, as they remained linked by ties of close friendship based on mutual respect, a friendship from which Webern benefited without taking actual lessons. Nevertheless, in the years which followed immediately after, Webern's feelings of friendship and gratitude to Schoenberg increased to the point – if it may be called so – of unconditional dependence, a feeling from which he suffered psychologically from time to time.

As already indicated, the year of the completion of the "Passacaglia" (1908) brought to an end the intensive lessons with Schoenberg. The young Webern, with his Ph. D. (1906), with his conscientious work on Heinrich Ysaac and his courses in composition with Schoenberg completed, and now a composer of several works to be taken seriously, urgently faced the demands of everyday life. Quite apart from the fact that his father, who depended on his salary as an official and had no private means, did not dispose of large sums of money, and that it became increasingly difficult for him to provide for his grown-up son according to his needs, the young Webern wanted independence. He now hoped to practise music professionally and slowly to stand on his own feet; particularly because when a young philosophy student – as he indicated in his diaries of 1904 – he had met his cousin Wilhelmine Mörtl, the daughter of a Viennese lawyer, and had fallen in love with her. They became engaged and hoped within the foreseeable future to found their own home. In order to do so, he had first to find a proper means of existence.

Webern took the longed-for step into practical musical work in the summer of 1908; he was given the chance of becomming second conductor of the Kurorchestra and chorus repetiteur, as well as deputy conductor, of the Bad Ischl Summer and Kurtheatre. Bad Ischl was then the summer residence of the Emperor, as well as that of many people of the court and of the aristocracy, so that a post at the theatre was not without interest. It is no longer certain who obtained this engagement for Webern. Similarly, the not unimportant question of where and how Webern acquired the necessary ability to conduct remains shrouded in mystery – even though he was later to become a successful, much appreciated and responsible concert conductor. It may be assumed that he never took regular lessons in conducting; nothing is known of his having taken instruction at a Konservatorium, or as a private pupil of some master conductor. Clearly his lessons with Schoenberg provided him with a knowledge of the general elements of music as well as with a more specialised knowledge of the analysis of form. On this basis the young musician dared to begin conducting and to work as a repetiteur although, it should be noted, in the not particularly exposed position of a minor assistant conductor in the little Upper Austrian spa of Bad Ischl.

Perhaps Webern's friend and colleague, Heinrich Jalovec – or other knowledgeable acquaintances – may have provided him with some hints on conducting. (Obviously, this was something quite different from what the eighteen-year old boy had imagined as the path to the conductor's desk.)

From the letters Webern sent from Ischl it is clear that he suffered from the novel requirements of practical conducting – that is, in a small theatre – and also since at that time he had no experience of practical routine. He had to learn every small aspect of his craft by experience, as often happens with self-taught musicians: he had to acquire much basic knowledge by trial and error and the demands of technical conductorship and that of a being a chorus repetiteur simply by practising them. (As a conductor, but not as a musician, Webern must be described as self-taught.)

This is probably the explanation for the extraordinarily depressed letter Webern sent from Ischl to Ernst Diez in Dresden on 17th July, 1908. It is incidentally, the last letter to survive from Webern's hand to this friend of his youth. In it he writes, among other things: ". . . I should be extraordinarily pleased if you were to come. You would lighten the stay in the inferno for me. My activities are horrible. I can find no words for a theatre such as this: Away with such bosh! What a good deed would be done to mankind if all operetta and similar light theatres could be annihilated. Then no one would imagine that he need write a 'work of art' of this nature. If, like myself, one has to cope with

this stuff all day, it's enough to drive one mad." Though
the same letter speaks elsewhere of the hopelessness of
composing in Ischl, Webern at the time had far-reaching
plans for compositions which he hoped to realise shortly.
It should be noted that these plans were directed towards
opera, an idea which Webern was later to discard. His
old admiration for Wagner clearly played a part, an
admiration that had remained with him since his Bayreuth experiences, even if that stimulus had been calmed
and clarified by Schoenberg's teaching of the laws of
construction and form of absolute music. It is a great pity
that no notes survive about these opera projects, and that
no sketches recall what Webern had in mind. It is quite
possible that, out of a sense of false shame or inhibition,
he destroyed such material in an attempt to wipe out the
traces of "youthful indiscretion". Yet, at that time, in
1908, he was clearly serious in his plans, as the letter we
have quoted of the 17th July showed. On this point he
writes: ". . . That you, dear friend, want to write an opera
scenario for me makes me glad. I think that I have
already written to you once that I have begun composing
Maeterlinck's 'Aladine and Palomidas.' This will be my
first opera. Schoenberg is very pleased. Your scenario
could then become my second opera. But I make these
conditions: no great procession, no battle, nothing that
needs 'illustrating'.

"I need only a few characters. No 'theatrical piece'!
To a certain extent that is what Maeterlinck writes. But
to go further – away with everything that is now called
'theatre'! The opposite! Do you understand me? If your

book is along these lines, I agree. Everything else is the greatest anathema to me".

We know no more than what this letter contains. As already mentioned, Webern did not keep a diary after 1906, and no other letters containing similar confessions are known. Webern's plans, outlined with such emphasis, such élan and such honest enthusiasm, led to no concrete results.

But to return to the external events of this period. Webern's first engagement as a conductor lasted several months – the length of the summer season – ending in the autumn of 1908, and the young musician returned to Vienna. Here he worked only occasionally as a conductor and chorus repetiteur.

But this period, which lasted until 1910, saw the composition of some important early works: the Lieder (op. 3) found their final form and were supplemented by the George-Lieder (op. 4, 1908–1909). Then he composed the well-known "Five Movements for String Quartet" (op. 5, 1909), followed by the first Orchestral pieces (op. 6) and the "Four Pieces for Violin and Piano" (op. 7), the two latter, belonging to the year 1910, being probably written in Carinthia during holiday periods.

It should be noted that the two books of Lieder still had their roots in the period of Webern's studies, but in their form and structure they already foreshadow some features of his later music. But now the composer began to base his style on the sound effects and possibilities of instruments, that is on the pure musical style which, aged between 25 and 27,

he found, developed and kept to. Later developments
did not basically add much that was new to these
characteristic, specific elements of style, except to vary
and modify them. This was entirely in in keeping with
Schoenberg's teaching, which probably became more
clearly rooted in Webern than in any other of Schoenberg's pupils. In their melodic and harmonic structure
the Lieder already show that Webern had gone beyond
tonality; the quartet pieces declare more clearly the very
personal language of the composer in the particular form
of stating and developing motifs.

There are no key signatures here to recall tonal links,
not even where, as a result of a subtle harmonic change,
a passing tonal relation might be indicated or constructed – an idea which, without doubt, the composer
did not intend. During this time, when Webern was
visibly striving towards independence – in the sense of
freeing himself from tradition – Schoenberg was also
beginning to overcome traditional tonality (1908–1910)
and to create music without the century-old laws of "the
theory of function". In 1908 Schoenberg completed the
second String Quartet (op. 10). The last two movements,
both with voice, and particularly the finale, are no longer
tonal. Then he completed the 15 George-Lieder from the
"Buch der hängenden Gärten" (op. 15), the piano pieces
(op.11), the orchestral pieces (op.16) and finally the mono-
logue. "Erwartung" (op. 17, 1909). In their construction
and planning, and in their concept of a new theory of
sound these works were something fundamentally new and
unusual for their time. Certainly Schoenberg, in some

ways, carried Webern with him in his highly experimental excursions into the new and unknown area of "music without tonal relations". He expected much from his pupil, who was devoted to him and whom he kept under his wing, even after the end of the actual "teacher-pupil" relationship. So it came about that the young Webern, infected and stimulated by Schoenberg's desire to experiment, looked for those elements which specifically appealed to him, and in this manner found a basis for his own new characteristic style. In the final instance it was to be very different from that of Schoenberg, even if its spiritual origins were never denied by Webern. The smallest motifs and parts of motifs, even "miniature motifs", which make up the substance of Webern's early works, remained typical of his style and of his musical expression at this time – in contrast to Schoenberg's new musical expression, which was more closely related to classical concepts. It was something absolutely new and remarkable.

More can be found about Webern's peculiarities of style in all his works – including those of the early period – in the special section devoted to his music. Here it need only be said that the years 1908 to 1910 helped Webern to find and work out the typical, specific elements of his style of expression.

These Vienna years, fruitful in their artistic, spiritual and creative aspects, were to be interrupted, even ended for a considerable time. The period had proved materially unrewarding: the young musician now faced the urgent need to obtain as soon as possible a position as a theatrical

conductor – one that could be developed, could be borne
and had good prospects. He had, after all, by now
acquired the necessary knowledge to manage such an
undertaking.

A chance offered itself at the civic theatre of Teplitz
(now in Czechoslovakia) for a brief engagement, which he
accepted. The only information on this point is a short
card sent to Alban Berg from Teplitz on 25th May, 1910:
"Dear Berg, I am quite happy here. I conducted the
'Geschiedene Frau', and shall shortly conduct three
further operettas. What about you? Will your quartet
be performed? Where will you be this summer?
Do write (Stadttheater Teplitz). With kind regards,
Webern."

Although to conduct "further operettas" was probably
not what Webern liked best, this relatively optimistic
postcard contains none of the usual complaints about the
theatre being an unbearable professional sphere, perhaps
because Webern regarded this summer engagement as
an exercise with a time limit.

This card is also remarkable for another reason: it is
the first addressed to the composer Alban Berg, his colleague of the fruitful and stimulating period of study
under Schoenberg. On the basis of many shared interests
during the Vienna period between 1908 and 1910 a warm
friendship had sprung up between the two. The two
friends were linked by common experiences, their shared
life and their admiration for Schoenberg, which approach-
ed the border-line of absolute psychological dependence.
Their admiration sometimes went so far as to submit to

Schoenberg's views even in their private affairs and personal attitudes.

But this is by the way. The fact is that for this period the short episodes in Ischl and Teplitz were to point the way – a painful way – for the next few years towards conductorships in theatres for Webern, who was then aged between 25 and 27.

The season of 1910–1911 saw him as assistant conductor at the Stadttheater in Danzig, probably as a result of a recommendation by his old friend and colleague at Schoenberg's lessons, Dr. Heinrich Jalovec, who then occupied the position of first opera conductor. As far as possible, he took care of Webern (he was to conduct operettas, rehearse the chorus and act as chorus repetiteur), but Webern was unhappy both about his job and the impossibility of composing.

In his letters to Alban Berg he allowed his despair free rein. Here, as an example, is an extract from his first letter from Danzig to Berg of 13th October, 1910.

"... Are you working much? In my case, alas, this is not so. I have much to do at the theatre. I conduct operettas, but the director has promised me 'Waffenschmied'* for the second half of November. But what is that worth? Here I am often in total despair, totally. It is disagreeable that there is nothing decent to eat (except by spending a lot of money). Life here is dear. The people highly disagreeable. I hardly ever get to the sea. That, naturally, is beautiful . . ."

Webern's letters from Danzig were all in this or a

* Opera by Albert Lortzing (1801–51).

similar vein. From the early part of his stay in Danzig onwards he hoped to leave for a holiday and never to return. The occasion was to be a concert of Schoenberg's pupils in Vienna, which Alban Berg was trying to organise. But it was not until April, 1911, that the longed-for concert materialised; in fact Webern obtained leave, travelled to Vienna, and did not return to his work in Danzig. After the Vienna concert Webern went briefly to Berlin to look for a new job. But apparently he lost his courage there; instead of returning to Danzig, he went to the home of his youth in Carinthia, to Klagenfurt, where he spent the summer. In the meantime his father had sold the "Preglhof" and Webern exchanged visits with Berg, who was staying at his family estate at the nearby Ossiachersee – after the painful year in Danzig Webern seems to have been thoroughly happy with his illicit stay in his own country.

The period in Danzig was to be important and fateful for Webern, even though artistically he gained nothing from it, since he was neither interested in the activities of the theatre nor enjoyed them. But on 22nd February, 1911, he married his cousin Wilhelmine Mörtl – having obtained a dispensation because of their blood relationship – and she bore him his eldest daughter, Amalie, in a Berlin clinic in April, 1911. Thus the foundation of Webern's family coincides with the unhappy Danzig period, and with it his life-long pecuniary difficulties became intensified.

Webern's contract with the Danzig theatre came to an end in the summer of 1911, and he never again visited

the town. We know no details of the ending of the
contract, but judging from later remarks in letters, the
affair seems to have ended not without its difficulties.
The composer's wilful departure seems to have brought
disagreeable consequences in its train. Nevertheless, in
spite of its many negative aspects, Danzig played an
important part in Webern's life.

After a summer spent in Carinthia convalescing, the
moment arrived when Webern had to look for a home
for his family. He neither wished, nor could remain for
any length of time in Klagenfurt as the guest of his father.
Nor could a basis for a reasonable existence be found
there.

But since his short stay in Berlin and his discussions
with agents there had remained without result, Webern
faced the end of the summer with nothing to look forward
to. With the help of Schoenberg and his brother-in-law
Zemlinsky,* who was then chief of the Prague opera, some
negotiations had taken place with the German theatre in
Prague. Yet Webern waited in vain for a definite reply
from Prague, at first in Klagenfurt, and after the end of
the summer in Vienna, where he was staying with his
father-in-law, the lawyer Mörtl (Ruckergasse 12, Vienna
XII). Then, unexpectedly, a letter arrived from Schoenberg, who had in the meantime taken an apartment in
Berlin in the hope of finding a sufficient number of
private pupils, apart from his position at the Stern Konservatorium. Berg and Webern agreed to try to collect
together rich patrons and lovers of the arts in Vienna,

* Composer, 1872–1942.

Berlin and elsewhere with the aim of establishing a
foundation for Schoenberg, to enable him to live without
financial worries. How seriously the two young composers sought to help support their beloved teacher
is clear from one of Webern's letters; it was written in
Vienna on 8th September, to Berg, who was still on
holiday.

"Your idea as regards Schoenberg is wonderful and we
must do everything to realise it. I am only afraid that
people's lack of energy will present difficulties. I spoke
to Stefan* yesterday. Naturally once again he has a thousand reservations. I believe that, above all, we shall have
to get Lincke** to take part too; he should write the
appeal for us. I shall write to him at once; our brochure
for Schoenberg should be published now. I don't know:
have you already sent your contribution? Do do it soon.
If I were to remain in Vienna we could easily achieve
this thing (your idea). Stefan is doubtful about the rich
people. But we do not want to doubt, we want to believe
that surely good people exist. In this way people's negative attitudes will be overcome. Something like this must
happen. Have I already written to you that, lately,
Schoenberg's project of moving to Berlin has taken on a
new lease of life? On September 15th an appeal is to appear in "Pan" composed by Fried*** and Kerr that pupils
should enrol (pointing out Schoenberg's importance),
which is to be signed by several Berlin notables. It will

* Paul Stefan, Viennese music critic.
** Pupil of Schoenberg.
*** Oskar Fried, conductor and composer (1871–1949).

be printed in all Berlin papers, and again in "Pan" on October 1st Clark*, a young Englishman in Berlin of whom I have already spoken to you, is all for it. He has visited rich people to help create a guarantee fund for Schoenberg (in case of his moving to Berlin). – Well, I should prefer it if we were to do well *here* so that all this would be unnecessary. But, in any case, if he can live better abroad than here, then he must go. I have no news yet from Prague. It may well take a few days. So I hope still to see you. –"

Schoenberg's departure for Berlin took place shortly after this. Soon Webern decided to travel to Berlin to be near his master, and also to take the opportunity of supporting the appeal for Schoenberg on the spot. Clearly, he hoped that he would find some sort of occupation in Berlin – as conductor, chorus master, repetiteur, etc., – to keep his head above water during what looked like a "dead year", as events were to prove. (Nothing had been heard from Prague). To be near Schoenberg helped Webern in many ways. A letter of 10th October, 1911, from Berlin-Zehlendorf, where Webern had recently found a home near Schoenberg's, provides some clues as regards Webern's feelings:

"Dear Berg, It is wonderful. I am utterly happy to be again with Schoenberg. We live in the country, on the edge of a wood. Something like the Berghof, but equally natural. I should like to ask you the following: I want

* Edward Clark (1888–1962) Later in charge of modern music broadcasts at the B.B.C. General Secretary and subsequently President of the I.S.C.M.

to enter for the "Staatspreis". Please find out at the Akademie when the application must be in (at the latest), and where I should send my compositions. Perhaps something has been put on the noticeboard in the Akademie. Actually, the prize is meant for students and music schools, but Schoenberg says that I also could enter. The prize is 1,000 Kronen; I believe time is short. Will you find out soon? Many thanks. Try to discover exactly what I have to do. – Since I arrived here I have been in almost uninterrupted conversation with Schoenberg. He is full of hopes about the appeal. Is there news about it? Schoenberg is in fine form: he lives well and cheaply. I am looking for an apartment; few are to be found here. If only you could be here!!! Please give your wife my kind regards. Write soon to Schoenberg's address. I shall soon write to you again. I am very sorry that I had to leave you! Your Webern."

Another letter of 12th October, 1911, to Berg is even more interesting in the light it throws on the situation. It deals rather more with Schoenberg's financial position than with Webern's interests – Webern having been the driving force behind the whole appeal to find support for Schoenberg, as is also shown by later correspondence from Berlin. Schoenberg's affairs dominated Webern's life during his year in Berlin from 1911–1912. Occasional earnings were few. Lacking evidence or witnesses, it is impossible to say what the Webern family lived on in Berlin. It is certain that they lived exceedingly modestly without many needs, so that probably the income from occasional work was sufficient for everyday life.

Perhaps, too, Webern still had some savings from his time
in Danzig, so that he was able to afford to go from Berlin
to Munich to the Mahler Festival with Berg. This
characteristic episode, which demonstrates the great
change undergone by Webern in his youth – probably
under Schoenberg's influence – from his critical attitude
towards Mahler's music should be mentioned here, particularly as Webern was to become an excellent and
thoughtful Mahler conductor. Webern wrote to Berg on
30th October, 1911:

"Dear Berg, On November 19th and 20th the Mahler
Festival is on in Munich. Yesterday, the 'Berliner Tage-
blatt' had the enclosed to say about Mahler's 'Lied von
der Erde'. Is it possible that we should not be there? A
new work by his hand for the first time since Mahler's
death. And we should not be there? Because of eight hours
in a train? Financially, it should be possible for us, don't
you think? I mean, for me it will not be easy, but it is
possible. In your case surely too. Time we have too, I
certainly. And you can take time. Without a doubt. Perhaps your wife cannot come and you do not want to leave
her; I leave my wife and child alone here. Do you think
of me as a bad man for that reason? I don't think I am,
yet nevertheless I am leaving my family alone. So you
can do it too. Particularly since your wife has her parents
nearby. Is there anything else that might stop us? I can
think of nothing more. And now for the things which
make me so excited that I can hardly wait to be in
Munich. When you have read in the enclosed cutting,
the end of the poem of the 'Lied von der Erde', do you

not, my friend, expect the most wonderful things from
the music – something so beautiful as has never existed
before? 'O my friend, while I was in this world my lot was
hard. Where do I go? I go and wander in the mountains,
I seek rest, rest for my lonely heart'. For heaven's sake,
what music there must be! I imagine that I can already
guess it before I hear it. Man, can you bear it? I can't.
They are also doing the 'Second', which I should like
to hear again. Last time I heard it under Mahler in
Vienna in 1907. Four years ago. How much four years are
at our age! Dear Friend, for the rest I am so looking forward to seeing you there. I would have so much to discuss
with you. We must arrange it so that we can hear some
rehearsals and both performances. You must make a
direct approach to Walter* in Vienna. You will want to
know when the rehearsals will take place, etc. Above all
get permission from him to attend the rehearsals. It will
also depend on Guttmann. We shall have to get tickets for
the performance from him. I am sure Schoenberg will
give a recommendation for you and myself. This will take
care of everything. I managed that way with the 'Eighth'.
I had free tickets for both performances, in spite of the
enormous crowd. I know of a cheap hotel. So it will cost
us only the journey and our stay. About 50 Marks, all
in all. Dear Berg, do let us do it. I ask you. If you do not
come, then I shall only half enjoy myself. Please write
at once what you think, so that we can arrange the details.
Tomorrow is the 1st of November! In a fortnight we

* Bruno Walter (1876–1962) Austrian conductor and famous
interpreter of Mahler.

must meet in Munich. Please do what you can to make it possible ..."

The two young composers also wanted to invite Schoenberg to Munich for the Mahler Festival, though neither had much money. Webern also spent at that period a great deal of time and trouble in preparing a brochure in Schoenberg's honour, to which all those of Schoenberg's pupils contributed who could more or less hold a pen. Finally, after many different attempts to find a suitable and willing publisher, it appeared under the imprint of Piper and Co. in Munich in the spring of 1912.

The contents table gives the following essays: A short biographical sketch of Schoenberg's life and development; a list of his works; "Introduction" (Carl Linke): "Schoenberg's music" (Anton von Webern); "The Treatise on Harmony" (Heinrich Jalovec); "The Pictures" (W. Kandinsky); "Schoenberg the Painter" (Paris von Guetersloh); "The Teacher" (a series of articles with contributions from the following pupils: Carl Linke, Dr. Egon Wellesz, Dr. Robert Neumann, Erwin Stein, Dr. Heinrich Jalovec, Dr. Karl Horwitz, Dr. Anton von Webern, Paul Koeniger, Alban Berg.) Here Webern's above-mentioned essay "Arnold Schoenberg, the Teacher" appears. This volume gave rise to a lengthy and complicated correspondence which occupied Webern for several months (from December 1911 to February 1912), practically to the exclusion of all private or professional activities; little that concerns Webern personally can be learnt from these letters. A specially bound copy was in fact handed to Schoenberg in Prague in February 1912 with the original dedication "To Arnold Schoenberg in greatest admiration".

In addition to work on the Schoenberg volume – which involved him in much editing as well as the writing of two essays – Webern completed in Berlin the Two Songs (Op. 8) on texts by Rilke for soprano and 8 instruments, which he had begun in 1911. In the period between 1908 and 1911 he had completed in Vienna the Five Pieces for String Quartet (op. 5), the Six Pieces for Orchestra (op. 6), and the Four Pieces for Violin and Piano (op. 7). As already mentioned this Viennese period more or less saw the birth of Webern's more definite personality as a composer.

The stay in the immediate and constant presence of his beloved master Schoenberg did not prove to be as stimulating and fruitful as Webern had hoped and expected. The fault may have been due to Schoenberg's overwhelming personality; he liked his disciples to "serve" him. So it is easier to understand Webern's willingness once again to accept a new post as a theatre conductor, an opportunity which arose in Stettin, where Webern spent a further year of joyless and artistically unproductive work. It is hardly surprising that he should have regarded this work simply as a continuation of that at Danzig, which brought him neither satisfaction nor enrichment; that this was so clearly appears from his plaintive letters written to Berg.

Webern left Berlin at the end of February 1912: for the moment the desired and also feared post of theatre conductor was still in the future. Why he left is not quite clear; we know only that he definitely appeared

in Prague at the end of February, probably in Schoenberg's entourage. Schoenberg, possibly as a result of
Zemlinsky's intervention, was there to rehearse and
conduct his "Pelleas", which he performed during the
latter part of February 1912. It was a success, and brought
Schoenberg an invitation to return in the near future, an
opportunity which Webern also took to return to Prague
with his master. It is possible, too, that Schoenberg
now presented his pupil at suitable places as a candidate
for the post of conductor at the Prague German Theatre,
then under Zemlinsky's musical direction. Schoenberg's
intervention did not at once bear fruit, yet it certainly
proved advantageous for Webern to be able to sound
Prague with the help of his teacher. Shortly after
the Schoenberg concert Webern returned to Vienna,
where his wife and child had arrived in the meantime.
At the end of March he received the Stettin contract,
which compelled him to begin work at the opening of the
summer season, on 1st July, but which meant his arrival
there as early as the end of May. Webern had resolved not to chance losing the Stettin post through
"flight" or "non-arrival", as in Danzig. But in the meantime he had undertaken the preparation of several concerts in Vienna with programmes of works by Schoenberg's
pupils. Some of his own compositions were to be played,
among them his Violin Pieces (op. 7) with Arnold Rosé.
The necessity of leaving early for Stettin appears to have
made it impossible for Webern to accompany his own
works, as he would much have liked to have done. He re-
signed from his Vienna obligations and visited his father

at Klagenfurt before leaving; from there he persuaded Berg to take over the task of preparing the concerts. This Berg fulfilled with great devotion to Webern's wishes.

Once in Stettin good intentions were replaced by acute homesickness, from which Webern increasingly suffered when abroad. On arriving in Stettin on 21st June, 1912, the first thing he did was to submit an application for leave to the directors, in order to travel briefly to Vienna, to attend the performance of his own compositions and those of the Schoenberg circle. His application was granted at once, as a happy Webern reported to Berg in a letter of 22nd June, 1912.

Generally, the atmosphere at the Stettin theatre was to prove depressing and hopeless for Webern, which, as indicated, produced a new outburst of complaints. Thus he wrote in his letter of 4th July, 1912 (to Berg):

"Dear Friend, I write to you in true despair. Here I occupy a terrible position. It is impossible to explain how I hate it all. I am filled by just one wish – away from here! I find myself surrounded by people occupied with ridiculous music; I am suffocating. In addition, I am so busy that there is no time for anything else. At the best there is just time to rest, which I need badly, because I am seriously ill. My nerves are in a terrible state. Everything has now gone to my feet. They hurt so much that I can barely walk. I don't know how I can bear it. But what shall I do? I am tied because of our expensive apartment. It would be simple to bring Stein* here as my successor.

---

* Erwin Stein (1885–1958), one of Schoenberg's earliest pupils. Author of "Orpheus in New Guises".

But what to do with the flat? (1,300 Marks, just think).
Perhaps it will get better in the winter. And the summer
passes so quickly. The summer shall pass quickly, that I
must hope for, I who live only in the summer. I must not
think of our estate, etc., or I shall pine away with longing.
My apartment is beautiful, but what's the use of that?
I want to leave, leave. For the mountains. There everything is clear, the water, the air, the earth. Here everything is sad. I am poisoned when I drink the water. If
only I were well, but what then? I feel tortured. Without
a thought, tied to my ridiculous work. I feel ashamed. I
can think of nothing good; I cannot occupy myself with
anything. Briefly, I am suffocating. Shall I tell you once
more what I wish? To live near Vienna on a small income,
dedicated to my real work. To undertake some other
work, give lessons, prepare piano scores. If only ambition
did not exist. Nevertheless, I have practically lost it, I
mean false ambition. All the same I should like to conduct
Mahler and Schoenberg. You see, I am again faced by a
dilemma. Above all, I wish to be well enough to be able
to work again. But I cannot get well in this job. Perhaps
I shall have to drop it. Possibly my body will revolt. It is
a shame, but so it seems . . . The thought makes me unhappy. I have the feeling that a lonely life, cut off, in an
area sympathetic to me alone will calm me. To feel so
down every day is terrible. Hence perhaps my depression
with everything here. But so it is. Why should I have
such a poor body? My dear friend, what a series of complaints! Do not be cross. But it calms me. Yesterday I
wrote in a similar way to Schoenberg . . ."

From other letters it appears that Webern was now doing fewer chorus rehearsals and more conducting, though mainly operettas. Above all he suffered from finding this form of art alien to his spirit, though he never forgot how much practical experience this "having to conduct at any price" provided him with, since every step towards the practice of conducting enriched his experience.

Naturally his lack of interest in the present narrow limits of his profession caused him much annoyance, which increased and deepened his hostility to Stettin and the atmosphere surrounding his position, though it provided him and his family with a reasonable income. Thus Webern wrote to Berg on 19th October, 1912: "I have just returned from the theatre, deeply disgusted. An operetta producer wiped the floor with me, like a dog. Because I arrived a few minutes late for rehearsal. You see, even such things happen. And now your letter arrived. With it you made me deeply happy. You are thinking of me, you love me. I thank you a thousand times, my dear friend. Because I am not a dog. . . . Tomorrow I will go to the doctor. I shall ask for leave and then away from here!"

It is almost self-evident that Webern's period in Stettin did not produce any compositions. Webern himself complained in almost every letter about the impossibility of composing. So the year spent in Stettin was significant only in the sense that it provided materially for the Webern family, and that it helped him to further the purely technical side of conducting, a fact he readily acknowledged.

(19th October) ... "Perhaps I shall manage to conduct concerts; perhaps also perform my works. The purely technical abilities I have now got ..."

(19th July, 1912) ... "I have now conducted several times, and much work awaits me. At least I am gaining experience of my craft. This is something at which I am working hard, and so aim to conduct as much as possible ..."

Anything less agreeable would be difficult to imagine for a highly strung creative man. As Webern did not see a chance of escaping from the atmosphere of the operetta, and as his only contact with the so-called spirit of serious music was that he was once permitted to conduct "Waffenschmied" (which he had already been promised in Danzig, though the promise was not fulfilled) it is not difficult to understand his degree of despair, particularly as he could neither find the time nor the necessary concentration to begin composing. In this vein he wrote on October 18th, 1912:

"... I have the following plan: I shall go to the doctor here, and if he thinks it necessary for me to rest, then I shall take immediate leave for a month. I should prefer a clinic, perhaps at Semmering, to recuperate. Then I shall go to Berlin. I want to give up the theatre. That is a firm decision. Things are going badly with me ..."

Many other letters tell of the difficulties Webern faced in his dealings with the world of operetta; for example this of 19th July, 1912.

"... Imagine how we feel when we think of such an operetta, and I have to take it seriously now. If I were not involved I should flee from a theatre such as this as from a plague spot; and here I've got to stir the sauce with them. I am often ashamed; I seem like a criminal to myself. To have to participate in this worst state of humanity! I can barely await rescue from this morass . . ."

These excerpts seem adequately to characterise the time spent in Stettin, a time when the composer faced the prospect of seeing his creative talent running out as a result of the daily demands made upon him. Only some visits to Schoenberg in nearby Berlin, or several short journeys to Vienna made it possible for him to keep himself psychologically above water. Then, during the early weeks of 1913, Webern put his plan mentioned in the summer of 1912, i.e. to take sick-leave, into action. He travelled to Vienna for a brief spell. A few weeks later, on 1st February, 1913, he wrote to Berg with various requests and suggestions from the select clinic of Dr. Vecsey, where, apparently at the expense of a now unknown donor, he underwent a thorough cure in order to restore his health. To complete the cure, he went immediately to Portorose in Istria, where apparently he felt at home in the maritime atmosphere, in spite of cold and inclement weather. But the rest and recuperation periods appeared insufficient. When, at the end of April, Webern returned to Austria, he first spent some weeks in Klagenfurt, and then, at the beginning of June, went to Mürzzuschlag, where he also spent July. He returned to Vienna in August to stay with his father-in-law (the lawyer Mörtl). A return to Stettin was not discussed. How Webern ended his contract with Stettin is apparent neither from any surviving

correspondence, no from any existing documents or witnesses. Anyway, it appears that the separation from Stettin was satisfactorily achieved; nothing was heard about
any return to the North German city (he seems in fact to
have used the desired sick leave to sever relations with a
place in which the atmosphere had become insufferable).
From the correspondence of the summer of 1913
we gather that Webern had entered into more serious
discussions with the "Deutsche Theater" in Prague, and
was looking forward to his arrival there.

Webern however did not leave for Prague. Once more
his phobia about the theatre held sway. It is this phobia
which makes Webern appear "work-shy" during the
period before the first world war, without his being so in
fact. To describe the situation in the summer of 1913,
before the opening of the theatre and concert season, we
quote this letter to Berg of 21st August, 1913:

"Dear Friend, Forgive me for being silent so long.
Until a few days ago my position was unclear. I had
much to think about and to write. Now things are as
follows: Zemlinsky urged me not simply to take 2–3
months leave, but to take the whole season. He wrote in
the most friendly way. Thus I decided to ask to break my
contract. The director agreed in a charming manner in
the hope that I would come the following year. So, for
the time being I am free ..."

One point seems certain. Basically, the expensive and
time-consuming cures and holidays at Semmering, on the
Adriatic, in Klagenfurt, in Mürzzuschlag, and last but not
least in Vienna, his beloved home, did not greatly help

him. He continues to complain in his letters about
his physical and psychological health, and was now compelled to seek treatment with a psychoanalyst. The same
letters also tell us of Webern's decision to look for and
rent an apartment in Vienna for his family and himself;
it was in Alt-Hietzing, not far from the homes of
Schoenberg and Berg, at the corner of the Kremsergasse
and the Fleschgasse. It was in this flat that Webern spent
the rest of 1913 and 1914, a period in which he composed
his 6 Bagatelles for string quartet, (op. 9), his 5 Pieces
for Orchestra (op. 10), and the Three Small Pieces for
Cello and Piano (op. 11). Today hardly any written documents of this period survive. Apparently, the correspondence with Berg ceased, since the two friends, who
were living as neighbours, preferred to meet and talk
rather than write.

Nothing of substance therefore testifies to Webern's
life during this period (1913–1914). Possibly, as earlier in
his career, he may have given lessons in musical theory and
worked as a repetiteur, which kept his head more or less
above water, until, in 1915, he had to join the army. The
first world war had broken out in the autumn of 1914.
Webern who had never served before, was not among
the first to be called up during this unhappy year. In
1915 fate overtook him, this totally unmilitary artistic
personality, who had volunteered for service with the
Red Cross. At first he was sent as a "Einjaehrig-Frei-
williger" (a young officer volunteer) for military training: it should be noted that the word "volunteer" must
be taken literally here, since Webern proved to be a

warm and uncritical patriot who swallowed wholesale
all the propaganda of the Austrian army. He was
saved by his eyes from actually having to fight at the
front for his ideals. From his earliest youth Webern
had had weak eyes and was shortsighted, and even as a
young boy had to wear strong glasses. Thus military
service was for him, apart from his military training,
office work in various quarters behind the lines. During
the short course at the officers' school which preceded
his military service, he first came into contact with sol-
diering proper.

But Schoenberg's fate rather than his own was dear
to Webern's heart at that time. He never grew tired of
suggesting that Schoenberg should be excused military
service, which was indeed achieved after some delays.
To illustrate Webern's passionate endeavours on behalf
of his beloved teacher, we reproduce here his letter to
Schoenberg's publisher, the Universal Edition in Vienna,
together with a letter which Webern sent to Berg from
his first military station, Goerz. Thus Webern wrote on
5th March, 1915, to the Director of the Universal-Edition,
Dr. Emil Hertzka:

"..... I write to you about Schoenberg. We must
achieve his release. I cannot understand that no one who
is able to do so, or at least has some influence, has made
representations in this sense. Arnold Schoenberg is allowed to wear himself down in military service, to ruin his
health, to waste his precious time. Dear God, does no
one understand what this means? It should be added that
Schoenberg is also suffering financially.

"As from today Schoenberg is stationed at Bruck an
der Leitha (School for Reserve officers). There his un-
suitability for war service will be discovered. But this
must not continue. Naturally, he does not tell anyone
how difficult he finds it. But I know that he is ruining
himself. Lehár was immediately excused military service.
That proves that it is possible to free Schoenberg. Of all
these others, Reger, Pfitzner, composers, conductors, etc.,
in Vienna, in Berlin, not a single one is serving. I beg
you, Herr Direktor, please support Schoenberg's release.
It is high time. I beg you most warmly! You too, Herr
Direktor, don't you feel how impossible it is for Arnold
Schoenberg to serve? It is a blot that he should have been
called up, whether in ignorance of his personality or in
spite of it. To remove a man like him from his work
is the worst kind of cultural damage the state can
suffer. If anyone is 'indispensible' then it is Arnold
Schoenberg . . ."

To Berg, Webern wrote on 20th April, i.e. some time
later, after nothing decisive had happened in the
Schoenberg affair:

"Dear Friend, just got your card. You seem to agree
with my view that at all costs Schoenberg's entry into
the army should be prevented. Well, then I cannot
understand why you should want Schoenberg's view
on this point. It is clearly 'no'. What must happen
here must happen even against Schoenberg's wishes. It
is impossible to ask him. What is Schoenberg to discuss
with Redlich or anyone else about being exempted from
military service? No, this must be done simply without

asking Schoenberg, even if he does not want it. Therefore, I am happy to hear from you that Loos* has already
taken some steps. I shall write to Loos. Perhaps it will be
possible to have Schoenberg declared 'indispensible'
(with the help of the Ministry of Education in Vienna
or the Academy). It must be done. At least have another
talk with Loos. But don't talk to Schoenberg in this sense
about his opinion!!! You must not mention our intentions
to him!!! He will say, obviously: 'Since I am called up
I shall come'. Yet, he wrote to me in connexion with
myself that the government should be concerned to
preserve and protect people with special faculties. What,
my nothingness compared with Arnold Schoenberg!! So
it must succeed. And Loos must take all steps at once
energetically and you must help. It just must be that way.
I am eating my heart out and can do nothing. So,
clearly . . . Even against Schoenberg's wishes . . Because
it is our task, that of the world, and no longer his."

A day later, on 21st April, Webern again airs his problems in a letter to Berg:

"Dear Friend, I wanted to add that quite apart from
our chief task of trying to free Schoenberg from military
service, we must not forget to secure an army job for
Schoenberg, which he wants to do in any case (fortress
artillery). I imagine that Schoenberg himself has perhaps
discussed this with Redlich and has already made en-
quiries in Vienna . . . I wrote to Loos yesterday, but spoke
only of trying to secure Schoenberg's exemption, and not
about securing an army job for him. Have you discussed

* Adolf Loos, Viennese architect.

this with Redlich? You know, basically I think and hope
for the safest thing of all: that Schoenberg will be
found unsuitable. But I have little hope. That's why we
have to be so careful ... Again Schoenberg must not know
of our intention to keep him out of military service. I imagine it like this: probably it will be impossible to prevent
Schoenberg from being called to the colours. But we
must make sure that, even if he should be found suitable,
he will be released from service. And if Schoenberg will
receive a letter from the authorities: 'Since you are
Arnold Schoenberg, you are exempted from military
service', he will be just as pleased as if he had been
called to the war, as if he had been called up. Dear
friend, no word about our correspondence to Schoenberg,
so that he does not guess what we are trying to do. I can
hardly express my burning desire to see a happy ending
to this case."

In Goerz Webern was compelled to lead a life in the
barracks without any privileges. In the circumstances
composing was out of the question, and so he had
to cross the military service years out of his artistic
life. Even the fact that he was moved to a small
place in southern Styria, Windisch-Feistritz, south of
Marburg, could not change that. From there Webern
wrote animatedly to Berg several times – a sign that, within the bounds of the possible, he was happy. But he did not
forget Schoenberg's military problem which, although
finally settled to everyone's satisfaction, continued to
occupy Webern's thoughts. In the course of his military
career, he went through several training courses –

in Frohnleiten near Bruck an der Mur, and finally in
Leoben in Styria, where eventually his military fate
was decided in his favour. As a result of his poor eye-
sight, at the beginning of October, 1916 he was down-
graded as "suitable only for 'Landsturmdienst' (Local
service) without arms."

"I am again regraded 'for local service without
weapons.' I was almost allowed to go. Because of my
eyes – they have become very bad," Webern wrote on
13th October, 1916, from Leoben. And on 22nd December
he reported, also from Leoben, that he would be completely freed as having been found "unsuited to all
Landsturmdienst (local service). On leave!" In fact,
this took place at the beginning of 1917, by which
time he had risen to the rank of officer-cadet. At
this point we find him furnishing his new flat in Alt-
Hietzing, Auhofstrasse 136, which was a short walk from
Berg's flat in the Trauttmandsdorffgasse 27 in the same
district. But he was not to be happy for long with his
newly won freedom from military service and his new
flat. On 2nd March, 1917, Schoenberg, now also happily
released from military service, and Webern went to
Prague, apparently for a concert or a lecture of
Schoenberg's, but also to reactivate Webern's engagement at the Deutsche Theater. It was arranged for the
summer season, and Webern returned to Vienna. But
soon, perhaps because of the appreciable difficulties
with food at that time, Webern exchanged Vienna for
the more countrified Klagenfurt. Thus, on 1st July, 1917,
a cheerful postcard reached Berg from Klagenfurt, which

showed Webern back at his task of composition. (The songs mentioned were later incorporated into Opus 13.)

".... here in Carinthia it is much better. Even if the heat and the drought give cause for serious worry. It is incredible: it has not rained since April. I am constantly thinking that, soon, I shall be back with the military. The next call-up will surely affect me. I expect it must be so. The war goes on. Often I think, so be it. To bury everything in oneself – to fight – one day there must be an end to it. The other day I heard for the first time artillery thunder from the front ... I am back at composing. At the beginning I experimented around a lot. Now I think that I have succeeded well with two orchestral songs. One: 'Wiese im Park' by Karl Kraus, one after the Trakl poem 'Abendland 3'. I hope it continues. At the end of July I return to Vienna. I still hope that Schoenberg will come here. I am expecting his news impatiently ..."

The impression made by this letter is deepened when compared with the first letter from Prague of 18th August, 1917.

"I am pining for the summer, i.e., the time when I was able to work. I have gone along the right paths. Schoenberg confirmed that. Already I am writing quite differently. I have composed four orchestral songs. Homogeneous sounds, partly long themes, altogether something quite different from before the war. I have felt it for some time. Now I should be good at composing. But I have to be in the theatre. I want it myself. Yet this permanent hindering of my work is most painful. My conscience

bothers me. We have a duty to compose. So I long for
you to gain the chance of writing . . ."

Webern's work in Prague, like all his earlier work in
theatres, did not last long. It seems to have ended in the
summer of 1918. Even the benevolence of Zemlinsky,
the man who had so carefully prepared the ground and
kept the post open for Webern, could not persuade him
to stay. Apparently in Prague, too, Webern was asked to
conduct operettas. What he actually achieved, musically
speaking, in Prague is not known. No reports about his
Prague period can be found. The fact is that by August,
1918 he was back in Vienna, looking for a new flat. This
he finally found in the historic* suburb of Mödling,
where he was to live until shortly before his death. At
the time, in 1918, Schoenberg also took a flat in Mödling:
and as always Webern wished for the physical proximity
of his loved and admired master. As a result Webern
and Schoenberg were separated by a walk of five minutes
– the latter in the Bernhardgasse in the southern quarter,
the former in the Neusiedlerstrasse 58. In the meantime,
in 1915, his son Peter had been born.

After the ending of the Prague period, the need to earn
money for his growing family become more serious.
In Vienna, he wished seriously to implement his earlier
decision to leave the theatre alone, and instead to work
as an orchestral conductor and teacher. The "Verein für
musikalische Privataufführungen" (Society for Private
Musical Performances) which Schoenberg had founded
and directed, provided him with an opening and a jump-

* Beethoven lived there towards the end of his life.

ing-off board. The "Verein" aimed at putting on musical works (especially contemporary music) rarely performed in normal concert programmes, and, with the help of careful rehearsals, to perform these well without having to take into account press notices or any other similar reactions. Entry to rehearsals and performances, usually in the Hall of the Club of Engineers and Architects in the Eschenbachgasse, was by invitation. In other words, only members of the Club, who were required to contribute fairly large amounts to finance these activities, and occasionally selected friends from Viennese musical circles, and finally well-known and interested guests from abroad were invited. No music critics or people who might be expected to report for newspapers were allowed in. In this manner Schoenberg had realised an ideal: that of perfect technical reproduction, which could never be achieved within the framework of ordinary musical life, governed as it was by commercial rather than by artistic, musical or spiritual considerations, and which was thus never free from snobbishness and tiresome personal vanities. Apart from the works of living composers of every artistic tendency, the works of dead composers were also played (such as Debussy or Reger – i. e. masters who might be regarded as the spearhead of contemporary music), with a careful accent on their stylistic peculiarities.

Composers who had their works performed in Schoenberg's Club could call themselves lucky. They could be certain that their music would be performed there in the manner they had intended, far removed from

the politics of success or any snobbish influence. For
this reason the audience was forbidden either to applaud
or to show displeasure, the press was excluded, and
published reports of performances of the club were not
welcomed. Performers, carefully chosen for their individual talent, were not, as in concert halls, the centre
of interest in the performance, but the servants of the
work to be given, which remained the main object
of careful labour. After discussions with his pupils
Schoenberg, whose personality allowed no concessions,
drafted the statutes and guiding lines of the "Verein".
In doing so he performed a cultural act which, in its
demand for cleanliness and concentration on essentials,
can still be recommended. Until 1922, i.e. for four years,
the "Verein" continued its existence. Then its place was
taken by the newly formed "Internationale Gesellschaft
für Neue Musik" (International Society for Contemporary Music) – a somewhat watered down version which
was poorer artistically and spiritually. In 1923 this staged
its first modern international Music Festival – the in-
heritance of the "Verein für musikalische Privataufführungen", which was the essence of the spirit of the
Schoenberg circle.

This was to be the spiritual atmosphere in whose
aura Anton Webern passed from the period of his
"Wanderjahre" (Years of Wandering) to a settled
existence from 1918 onwards. Schoenberg well knew
what he was doing when he called Webern – a man
who practised the utmost exactness, was sometimes almost pedantic, but at the same time religiously dedicated

to his art – into the inner circle of close collaborators
of the "Verein". His precision appeared to him the
best guarantee for a clean performance of those works
which he considered worth while within the framework
of his "Verein". And this was true for all works, whether
they stemmed from Schoenberg's school and its disciples,
or were quite different, even diametrically opposed (such
as those from the hands of Reger, Debussy or the followers of Wagner).

Thus in Schoenberg's "Verein" Webern became "master of performances", i.e. a sort of director of studies. He
supervised the choice of suitable interpreters, the lay-out
of rehearsals and similar matters, but did not concern
himself with the programmes as such, since Schoenberg
kept this task in his own hands. It is clear that Webern
gained as many advantages from this work as did the
"Verein" from his activities.

It is obvious that so idealistic an undertaking as
Schoenberg's "Verein für musikalische Privataufführungen" could not look forward to a long and successful
life in Vienna at that time. Schoenberg had thought of
liquidating the "Verein" as early as 1920, after all his
attempts to save this extraordinarily welcome undertaking – such as a rise in the already appreciable mem-
bership fees – had failed. But it was not until 1922 that
the "Verein" finally ended its activities.

This kind of work now ceased for Webern. But he had
learnt much which was to stand him in good stead in
mastering future tasks. In the meantime he concentrated
on finishing various compositions, which he had begun

or planned immediately after his military service, for example the Lieder (op. 13) for soprano and 13 instruments whose beginnings go back to 1914. (Texts by Bethge, Karl Kraus, Georg Trakl). The year 1917 (immediately after his military service), also saw the completion of the four Songs with piano (op. 12) using texts of a traditional song, Bethge, Strindberg and Goethe – a work which predates his departure for the Prague engagement.

1918 saw the passing of the law in Austria which abolished all old aristocratic titles. Nevertheless, the composer was occasionally, even in programme announcements, referred to as Anton von Webern.

On 10th August, 1919, after long and serious illness, Webern's father Dr. Carl von Webern died in Klagenfurt aged 69. The death of his father moved Webern, even though there had been differences between father and son from time to time, particularly during his youth, concerning the choice of his profession. Later the two had come closer again, undertaking joint excursions into the mountains and discovering many common interests.

And so Webern felt greatly the death of his father. To the elder Webern, the conservative official, faithful to his Emperor, the collapse of the rich and powerful Austro-Hungarian Empire, and the emergence of the new First Austrian Republic without the old ideals, must have been a severe blow, perhaps even a cause of his early death. Probably to have lived on in the new republican atmosphere would have had no meaning for him.

For Webern, 1920 was to see a revival – if a brief one –
of his activities at the Deutsche Theater in Prague; but
this activity with Zemlinksy, who had not forgotten him,
lasted only a few weeks, from the end of August until the
beginning of October. This was probably due to Webern's
inability to maintain two households out of his modest
income as a conductor – the flat in Mödling, where his
family had been increased by the birth of a third
daughter Christine in 1919, and his own flat in Prague.
Thus Webern again took the first chance of ending his
obligations in Prague and returned to Vienna.

Back in Vienna he added several agreeable features
to his life, which were to be useful to him later. Above
all, there was his first agreement with a publisher, the
Universal-Edition in Vienna, to publish the following
works: Passacaglia (op. 1), Chorus, Entflieht auf leichten
Kaehnen (op. 2), Lieder (op. 3), Orchestral Pieces (op. 6).
Schoenberg had played the part of an intermediary here
with the Director of Universal-Edition, Dr. Emil
Hertzka; quite apart from his high regard for Webern's
gifts, he was grateful for the role Webern had played
in easing his (Schoenberg's) military service. Like almost
all the composers of the Schoenberg school, Webern was
to remain linked to Universal Edition as a composer, and
later as reader and collaborator. He published all his
works with them, much stimulated by the positive and
progressive attitude which Dr. Hertzka displayed towards Schoenberg and his pupils. Also about this time
(1920) several important pupils began to arrive in
Webern's home, so that slowly his life in Mödling began

to find a more solid material basis. Or rather, the new
source of income contributed to the existence of his large
family, since to begin with the modest fees did not cover
the household expenses. For these, the small savings of
earlier years (military service and his theatre activities)
had to contribute.

During the following year (1921) Webern was to
receive additional help: he was appointed conductor of
the famous Vienna "Schubertbund", and also took over
the "Mödlinger Männergesangverein" (Mödling male
voice choir) as chorus master. These activities did not
last long – the first until 1922 and the second until 1926.
But in the meantime Webern's name became known and
appreciated, so that there was no longer any danger that
he would remain unoccupied.

Probably as a result of Schoenberg's intervention,
Webern was invited to Düsseldorf in the summer of
1921 to conduct his "Passacaglia" at the "Deutsche
Tonkünstlerfest". His first appearance abroad as conductor was quickly followed by a second, in June, 1922.
Webern was invited to Berlin to conduct a concert of
new Austrian orchestral works: Bittner, Schoenberg,
Webern. Shortly afterwards, in the autumn of 1922,
he was invited to take over the "Vienna Workers'
Symphony Concerts", founded in 1905 by Dr. David
Josef Bach, an activity which was greatly to satisfy
him and to which he brought much interest and
energy. At last the musician who in his youth had been
compelled to rehearse and conduct operettas in several
German provincial theatres – as he had written from

Stettin on 23rd September, 1912, to be "a jack of all
trades in the theatre" – had reached the stage of which he
had dreamt during all those years, i.e. to conduct concerts including the music of Mahler and Schoenberg. In
his capacity as conductor of the Workers' Symphony
Concerts he was able to contribute to the programme
planning. The aim of the Workers' Symphony Concerts to present an outstanding forum for modern
music – the music of Schoenberg and his pupils and of
other living or interesting and rarely performed composers, including Mahler – was due in the first instance
to Webern. He was able to put his ideas into practice,
mainly as a result of his friendly relations with Dr. Bach.
Thus these concerts were to become almost a branch of
the I.S.C.M. (International Society for Contemporary
Music) in later years. He found it possible to stage here
first performances of new orchestral works which would
have been too expensive for the modest budget of the
I.S.C.M. In this way the Workers' Symphony Concerts
achieved several aims: the cultural one of founding a
forum where the new, younger and little known composers could be heard beside the best music of all periods.
In the twenties, at a time when the general public showed
a negative attitude towards modern art, this was of para-
mount importance. Secondly the educational one, in
which an uneducated working class was presented with
contemporary works side by side with the classics and
the romantics, which were thus thrown open to discussion.
The educational aim was Webern's idea. Without being
active politically, he found himself naturally on the side

of progressive forces. Thus the two branches of Webern's idealism were united into one fruitful endeavour. Here too Webern the conductor, who had developed a rounded personality in this period, discovered a large and stimulating field for his activities.

As a conductor he scanned the works he was to interpret for days and even weeks of intensive study, using a method of formal analysis that he had acquired from Schoenberg's theoretical lessons. Naturally, he wished to pass this knowledge on to the orchestral players, but, unexpectedly, contact in this sense proved impossible. Generally, orchestral players fail to appreciate a detailed analysis of a score; they tend to play everything "at sight", as an almost unconscious routine, without further reflection about inner connections or reasons. According to his brother-in-law, Professor Wilhelm Gross, who frequently played in his orchestra, Webern always explained and talked too much while aiming to clarify. Thus the orchestral players did not take to a mentality foreign to their ways. Usually he failed to notice if at times people laughed at him, even if good-humouredly. It was a poor reward for a man filled with idealism and a sense of serving art. It was impossible for Webern to discipline the orchestra harshly or decisively, as may have been necessary from time to time. In spite of the difficulties during rehearsals, the performances left a fine impression. Everyone gave of their best; and during performances his manner of conducting and his way of transmitting his thoughts were impressive, even if his gestures (certainly unconscious and not studied) seemed to some exaggeratedly ecstatic. Although he never conducted without a score, he knew and mastered every note of the works performed. Conducting was an enormous physical and mental strain for him. Especially when conducting his own works, he used himself up and at the end of the concert left the conductor's stand pale and exhausted.

From this it will be seen that conducting for Webern came from the heart. His striving for the complete intelligibility of works, which he put at the service of modern music or Mahler's scores, did not suit his time and his environment, and so met with little understanding. Here the appreciation of the few understanding musicians had to console him for the lack of a wider comprehension among a broader public. Thus Webern could never become the great spoilt darling of the public, a real star, which in his youth he might have dreamt of. But, and for the true musician this may be the most important factor, it could be sensed from Webern's personality and his conducting that for him the pure, the factual and the real were what mattered. It was this which rendered him lovable.

In contemplating the picture of Webern as conductor these thoughts are uppermost. Especially those who sang in the chorus under Webern still think of him, and of all he was able to communicate musically and spiritually, with admiration and gratitude. He had become chorus master of the I.C.S. "Arbeitersingverein" (Workers' Choral Society) in 1923. And it is the members of this chorus, most of whom were amateurs, who partic-

ularly remember Webern's activities as a leader and as
an educator; which seems to underline his special talent
for inspiring people's choruses. (Webern kept the
post of director of the "Arbeitersingverein" until 1934,
i.e. until the dissolution of the Austrian Social Democratic Party.)

A further episode of 1922 is worth noting, since
Webern was its focus. The Vienna "Konzertverein" –
then one of the most important musical societies in
Vienna – engaged him to conduct its subscription
concerts. (The Society had an orchestra of the same name,
a predecessor of the present Vienna Symphony
Orchestra.) But suddenly difficulties appeared which
are described in this letter:

"Mödling, 11th September, 1922. Dear Friend (Berg),
I must now tell you something at which I have twice
hinted: at the end of August, I received a contract from
the Konzertverein, which contained clauses that had
never previously been mentioned; fourteen days' notice,
etc., and this after I had reached a definite verbal agreement with the President on a quite different basis. That
was before the summer. Of course I spoke to you when we
last met. I pointed to that agreement and refused this
contract. After some lengthy toing and froing, on my
side a meeting with the President in Grundlsee, and on
his with the Secretary and myself here in Vienna, we
finally agreed the following (a point on which Schoenberg and also Zemlinsky had advised me). I shall appear
at the first concerts as guest conductor. The papers will
state that I have been invited, etc., After three concerts a

decision will have to be reached whether I am to conduct
for the season, or whether it is to end. What goes on here
in Vienna is really horrible. The whole thing is without
a parallel. First a definite agreement, then conditions.
Finally a definite agreement torn up. (I also was tied by
it.) To start with, the whole thing seemed like a dangerous
feverish dream. Then it seemed to be not so. At least one
assurance, but of a formal nature only. So that I finally
agreed to this sort of trial conductorship. For the public
it is hardly that: I am invited to conduct three concerts.
More when we meet. The first concert is to be on the 17th
(this Sunday). But because of the printing strike it will
probably take place a week later. My programme:
1) Overture: The Mastersingers; Schubert in B minor;
Beethoven's Fifth. 2) Mozart's Jupiter, Wagner's Siegfried Idyll, Bruckner's 4th. 3) Beethoven's Coriolan,
Beethoven's Violin Concerto (the leader*), Brahms No. 1.
How much I should like you to hear one or other of these
concerts. But will you be back?".
Among other events of 1922, his appointment as choir-
master of the "Arbeitersängerbund" should be mentioned, since his post as Chorus conductor and trainer
was to prove the element that permitted Webern's specific
talents in musical teaching to unfold. Here he showed
his best, a best that was well above the average.

Webern developed a specially close relation to the
human voice. This was demonstrated by his undoubted
talent as conductor and teacher of choruses and also by
his special love for composing for voice, from which

* as soloist.

he demanded the most difficult things. This comes out in his compositions of the period. The works published up to this time can be divided into two groups: the Chorus (op. 2), the sets of songs with piano (op. 3, 4 and 12) and the songs with instruments (op. 8, 13 and 15) were written for voice; for instruments alone his compositions were the Passacaglia (op. 1), the string quartet movements (op. 5 and 9), the orchestral pieces (op. 6 and 10), the violin pieces (op. 7) and the cello pieces (op. 11), of which some – op. 10, 11, 5 and 9) – are of an aphoristic brevity.

However difficult the approach to Webern's music might then have been, the year 1924 brought the first real official recognition of his work. This was to be, however, more for the tireless organiser of the choir of the Vienna Arbeitersingverein than for the "odd and difficult" composer whose honest personality, and especially his ability, commanded the greatest appreciation, stemming as it did from a "traditional" background. In 1924 he was awarded the Music Prize of the City of Vienna (Webern was then 41), which for that time and for Webern's particular circumstances represented a not ungenerous amount, ten million Kronen (10,000 Schilling). In Webern's diary, which the composer was keeping in a sketchy form, the presentation of the music prize is noted laconically; in addition he carefully notes that during the year (1924) almost all his works completed by that date had been published by the Universal-Edition. This publishing house took Webern's works completely seriously, and he in turn, at Schoenberg's suggestion, had made a permanent contract with them. The service rendered by these publishers needs to be all the more appreciated, since at that period the publication of such music did not go hand in hand with profits!

The diary for 1924 also briefly notes Webern's journey in July to the music festival at Donau-Eschingen. There the 6 Bagatelles for string quartet (op. 9) (played by the Hindemith-Quartet) and the Trakl Songs (op. 14) (played by a Vienna Ensemble) were given their first performance. According to the diary, the Sacred Songs (op. 15) for soprano and chamber ensemble were performed for the first time on 9th October, 1924, in the Vienna Secession, by the soprano F. Hüni-Mihacsek and members of the Vienna State Opera orchestra. The diary notes, whose absence for the years 1906 to 1924 is to be greatly regretted, allow a clearer impression of the years after 1924. For the period without diaries it is difficult to reconstruct the life of the composer, even if existing correspondence or the memories of those who took part in some of the events are consulted.

To 1924 also belong the Five Canons for soprano, clarinet and bass clarinet on latin liturgical texts (op. 16). It was Webern's last work written outside Schoenberg's strict twelve-note technique, in which he practises, in spite of strict contrapuntal canonic writing, a so-called "free atonality". The same year saw Webern's official endorsement of Schoenberg's "Theory of composition with 12 notes related only to one another", or put more simply, a composition built and ordered according to a predetermined use of all the twelve chromatic notes, in a definite, consequential sequence or its mirror forms.

Naturally, it is impossible here to explain briefly the principles of twelve-note row composition. For more detailed information on the technical rules of composition of the Schoenberg school, if the reader requires them, it is necessary to consult more specialised literature.* But one thing is certain: Webern's first attempt at composing a single piece with a twelve-note row took place in 1924, in the form of the 3 Volkstexte (op. 17) for soprano, violin (or viola), clarinet and bass clarinet – a composition which still handles the twelve-note technique in a rather naive and primitive way.

Neither the quality of the texts Webern set (simple, popular, sacred lyrics with a primitive stress on the cult of Mary), nor his specific musical style and language decisively changed as a result of his adoption of strict, concessionless twelve-note music. (Webern, incidentally, specially loved sacred folk texts, particularly during the middle period of his creative development.) From this can be seen the extent to which he adopted as his own the specific properties of the musical language which emanated from the Schoenberg school, and that he developed his own musical expression, divorced from tonal functions, by himself, before any definite laws about composition with twelve-note rows had been formulated. Thus Webern's compositions use from the early opus numbers wide melodic intervals, rooted in Schoenberg's treatment of writing for voice, as shown in the spoken voice part (Sprechstimme) of Pierrot Lunaire, in its widely leaping sung declamation. From there the inter-

* Josef Rufer, Composition with Twelve Notes, London 1954.

vals were also used in instrumental lines, and became an
integral part of the style and form of the Schoenberg
school, which naturally received its characteristic expression from the pen of each individual composer. Webern's
specific harmonic and melodic style, according to his
individual invention and feeling, was always dominated
by intervals of major sevenths and minor ninths. Naturally it was easy to keep these characteristics (which anti-
cipated future developments) within the framework of
serial construction and to develop them. It should be
stressed here that the predominance of major sevenths
and minor ninths over smaller singable intervals existed
in and was dominant in Webern's music *before* Schoenberg's system of composing with twelve notes was discovered.

The observer may rightly assume that Webern's development as a composer was along an organic, logical and
clear path. Intuitively, he seemed to have sensed the
development, possibilities and laws of composition with
twelve notes. Thus no new components appeared in
Webern's music as a result of Schoenberg's "Composition
with twelve notes related to one another". Instead, almost
from the beginning (i.e. from the start of the period when
his music ceased to be dominated by tonal functions) until
the end, his composition progressed logically and uni-
formly, in all its components and in its particular stylistic
expression. (Here I should like to refer to the book
"Weberns Kompositions-Technik" by Dr. Erhard Kar-
koschka, which points to several interesting and original
features in this field.)

As far as Webern's biography from 1918 is concerned
– apart from his compositions – it is essential to deal with
his spiritual development as well as his philosophy, since
those who knew him stressed its importance. These years
show him first as a husband and father in the setting of
an almost petit-bourgeois background. Basically, Webern
was a devout man, less in the sense that he often went to
church, or demonstrated his religious beliefs to a wide
public, than in his inner spiritual attitude. For example,
after 1918 he carried with him as spiritual nourishment,
besides Goethe's "Faust", a copy of the Bible, which he
particularly enjoyed to read out of doors to show his
specific attitude in serving God. In line with this inner,
"pious", Christian and Catholic attitude he held his
family in high esteem. For him they were the people
nearest to him, who needed him and to whom he devoted
himself. Although Frau von Webern lacked artistic and
musical education, her husband accorded her his complete confidence, in musical matters as well. Webern
completely accepted her instincts in taste and according
to several people who knew the family well they were
seldom wrong. Whenever he had a new idea, or was
working on a new concept, he asked his wife to come to
his study (at any time of day) to play her his musical
ideas: she was the first person to hear them and he discussed all details of the new work with her. According to
friends it was touching to observe Frau von Webern
trying to keep up with her husband, so that some believed
here was a wife who really "understood" her husband
and his work, his philosophy, his technique, his ideas

and his most secret thoughts. Unfortunately, Frau von Webern's lofty character prevented her from speaking about her spiritual relationship with her husband, even to her children or her most intimate friends. Today, after the death of Frau von Webern in 1948, no one can be certain what she and her husband discussed regarding his work and his views on art.

To his children Webern was a good, loving father with an ever-open heart for their troubles. He even shared their school worries with them, and always tried to ameliorate or remove them. But he found little artistic understanding in his children, who were never able fully to follow their father's particular philosophy. If he was away, as was frequently the case in later years, (concerts, mountaineering), Webern wrote to his family almost daily, and always tried to keep the closest contact with his children, whom he dearly loved. At the same time, while working he insisted on complete peace at home, and always regarded household noises as upsetting his concentration. This may have given rise to an impression of Webern as a "household tyrant", which in fact was untrue.

In this connection it must be stressed that Webern, in spite of his predominately spiritual attitude, never appeared to be a man who had turned his face away from the world, an eccentric, or in any way peculiar. Within the modest limits he set himself he had time for the so-called "earthly pleasures", i.e. good food and drink, and he especially loved nature and its joys. Since his early youth he had enjoyed long and sometimes difficult walks and excursions, sometimes alone and sometimes in company, from which he returned happy and enriched.

The next few years, probably the most fruitful of his life, must be set against this background. In addition to the various posts so far noted, from 1926 he also held a position as teacher at the "Vienna Jewish Institute for the Blind", which he occupied with his usual conscientiousness. The salary was welcome to the Webern family, who were still far from well off. After a reduction of his activities as conductor, or at least a specialisation in this field, his main source of income came from teaching. For the sake of completeness some names must be mentioned here of those who enjoyed Webern's teaching and who in some cases, have continued and developed it. They are the composers Ludwig Zenk, Dr. Leopold Spinner and Julius Schloss, the teacher Prof. Erwin Ratz, the musicologist Dr. Willi Reich, the American viola player of the Philadelphia Orchestra Moritz Kaplan, the conductors Prof. Hans Swarowsky and Dr. Karl Rankl, the pianist Prof. R. Hauser, the harpsichordist Christa Fuhrmann and many others.

The years 1924 to 1932 are covered by Webern's diaries, from which some quotations are given here. No fundamental events were to influence Webern's personal life during this period. His life in Mödling, in moderately secure surroundings, with a fairly regular income and freed from the hated theatrical atmosphere, offered few climaxes, yet was nevertheless pleasant. In this way, in Webern's characteristically slow, careful manner of working, several new larger and smaller works came from his pen: he retained a style that had by then been developed and worked out, but for the present did not add any new components. The Universal-Edition published almost his complete works as he wrote them. Thus, in the laconic diary entries for 1925 one, similar to the rest, reads: 31st January, 1925: Completed Revision of my Lieder op. 8 and 13. In January: Handed over Lieder op. 12 to UE. In February: Handed over Lieder op. 8 and 13 to UE.

New compositions of 1925 are the Lieder (op. 18) for soprano, E flat clarinet and guitar, which Webern had specially composed for the publishers' Jubilee edition, as part of a collective effort by all composers then published by UE; these he dedicated to Dr. Emil Hertzka, who had done so much for him.

For the beginning of May 1926 his diary reads: "Gave up my post as choir master with the Mödlinger "Männer-Gesangsverein". Unfortunately he does not report what caused him to give up this post; in any case the cessation of this modest income was disagreeable for the Webern family. As a result Webern's friends (led by Alban Berg), as often before, jointly helped to save him from temporary material difficulties. Some help also arrived in the shape of an invitation to the I.S.C.M. Festival in Zurich (June 1926) to rehearse and conduct Schoenberg's Wind Quintet (10 rehearsals) and also his own Orchestral Pieces (op. 10) (7 rehearsals). Entry in diary as "Good performance of my piece (June 23). Impression of Swiss landscape: exhibition, not country! No gradual but considerable difference between East and West Alps".

For the rest 1926 proved important and propitious for Webern, as he succeeded in reaching a favourable and hopeful agreement in December with the director of UE, Dr. Hertzka; it meant that from that time the publishers paid Webern a monthly sum which was regarded as an advance. The same year also saw the beginning of his friendship with Hildegard Jone, who was later to write many of his texts, and her husband, the sculptor Josef Humplik. For 1927 the amount payable by UE was fixed at 1,200 Schillings, which eased Webern's material position again. Otherwise, from his diary notes it can be seen that, from the middle twenties, Webern's name began to appear more frequently in international concert programes – in contrast to Vienna, where he encountered difficulties in getting his compositions known.

It meant a growing income for Webern (who was a member of the AKM – Austrian Society for authors, composers and musical publishers) and also his publishers. In 1927 the Austrian radio named Webern as a regular conductor and asked him to take charge of a series of orchestral concerts; in this era of direct transmission these were usually given in the mornings, or occasionally in the evenings. Here Webern had a chance to exercise a decisive influence on the programmes. His Passacaglia (op. 1) was once (1930) performed in them. 1927 saw the completion of his String Trio (op. 20), an important work written strictly within the twelve-note technique, with a transparent structure (three solo strings) which accorded completely and without difficulty to the strict rules of the twelve-note concept, especially in the form of the work, which is the first of a series of compositions in two movements. These include the Trio, the Symphony (op. 21) and the Saxophone quartet (op. 22). Webern noted the completion of the Trio in his diary during his summer holiday in 1927, which he spent in the small resort of Hafning near Leoben in Styria, which with its rich view of mountain scenery suited his taste particularly well: " ... after much thought a difficult decision: to end work on the third movement of my string trio and to be satisfied with two movements. Clean copy of both".

In any case the stay in Hafning is interesting, since Webern's diary contains a note about the daily arrangements characteristic of his holidays. "Tried to begin work at eight o'clock in the morning. In fine weather went straight from bed to bathe in the Krumpenbachl. Work until about one o'clock. Staying in one's room not pleasant, cold and damp, a bit cellar-like on hot days. After lunch rested in the meadow behind the house, an hour at most. Sometimes went bathing with Minna and the children. Then work until teatime. Sometimes also later. After six o'clock, usually a walk in the Krumengraben or its surrounding woods, looking for fungi or berries." At the end of 1927 (November) the diary notes the publication of the Trio (op. 20); its first performance took place on 16th January, 1928, played by the Kolisch Ensemble in the Small Musikvereinssaal in Vienna.

At the end of April 1928 the Five Canons (op. 16) and the Two Songs for chorus and instruments on texts of Goethe (op. 19), composed in 1926, were published. In

February the earlier (1918) Instrumental Songs (op. 13) were given their first performance in Winterthur and Zurich. The summer, spent in Mödling, saw the completion of the Symphony (op. 21) which was left "after careful reflection" in two movements. Webern reorchestrated his Orchestral Pieces (op. 6), since he wished to rewrite the score more transparently and more economically (end of August to 4th September, 1928). Both works – the new Symphony and the rewritten Orchestral Pieces (op. 6) – were immediately sent to the Universal-Edition for printing and preparation of the orchestral parts. At the end of 1928 Webern was found to be suffering from a gastric ulcer, which forced him to cancel several concerts important to him (Festival of the Republic, Schubert Festival) and to seek a cure in the clinic of Semmering (probably with the aid of a patron).

It was not until January 1929 that he was able to return to his teaching and conducting activities. He had the satisfaction – a proof of the growing international acknowledgement of his activities as a composer – of being asked at the beginning of June by the American "League of Composers" to write a work for chamber orchestra for them. For it he received an honorarium of 350 dollars. After some reflection he offered his Symphony (op. 21) in two movements (for small chamber ensemble; clarinet, bass clarinet, 2 horns and strings) which had been completed shortly before and which had remained unperformed. On September 20th Webern noted in his diary: "Just heard that the New York "League of Composers" has taken my Symphony (op. 21) for first performance.

They had asked for a work from me. I suggested that they accept the symphony for this purpose. The offer amounts to 350 dollars". At the end of the year (November 15th) Webern undertook for the first time a major concert tour as conductor of works by other composers (Mozart, Hugo Wolf, Johann Strauss, Brahms, Schoenberg, Milhaud, Mahler), which took him to the B.B.C. in London via Munich, Frankfurt and Cologne; he returned to Vienna on December 4th. Altogether Webern was in London four times as visiting conductor; in the late autumn of 1929, in the spring of 1932, the spring of 1933 and the spring of 1935.

To show the effects which the events of a fairly long voyage and a stay abroad had on Webern, here are his diary notes for the first trip in the autumn of 1929.

"Friday, November 15: Began my trip to Munich, Frankfurt, Cologne, London. Left station at 11 o'clock in the morning. Feelings of happiness. Love for my country. Special impression: station restaurant Salzburg (arrived at 8 o'clock in the evening). Farewell to my country.

Saturday, November 16: Afternoon, 4 – 5 o'clock, first rehearsal in Munich. Schoenberg's "Verklaerte Nacht". Spent Sunday and Monday with Kaltenborn. Sunday at the cinema. Very unhappy impressions!

Tuesday, November 19th: Second rehearsal in the morning. Programme of the Concert.:

In the Tonhalle, 8 o'clock in the evening.

1. Mozart: Jupiter
2. Schoenberg: Verklaerte Nacht

3. Wolf: Italian Serenade
4. Johann Strauss: Tales from the Vienna Woods.

---

1. Strings better than in Vienna.
2. Very good.
3. Quite neat, clear, solo viola poor. Nevertheless generally well shaped.
4. Enjoyed it. Orchestra followed well; above all in making music. General form probably very good.

The programme put together as a result of much pressure (Title: German masters of the opera and the concert hall). But efforts richly rewarded. Result was important. Feeling of appearing for the first time abroad, exclusively conducting the works of others: rapid contact, thus happy. Not a trace of nervousness, fright. Surer than at home (Vienna). Much joy, felt well.

Lived in Hotel Eden, very pleasant. (First night elsewhere, a horrible spot). Ate at Kaltenborn's, was greeted by him at the station. First dinner in restaurant (Pschorrbräu). The last after concert with FK in hotel "Deutscher Kaiser". Excellent. Whole stay very pleasant. Nothing upsetting. Munich a beautiful town but provincial. Snow has fallen between Munich and Salzburg. Winter weather in Munich. Clear and frosty. Got on well with orchestra. Wednesday November 20. Left at 8 in the morning for Frankfurt. Arrived in the afternoon at 4. Was met by Wiesengrund*, went at once to Seligmann, where I was

---

* Theodor Wiesengrund–Adorno, pupil of Berg, critic and composer, b. 1903.

put up splendidly, and at once provided with delicious food.

Thursday, November 21 and Friday, November 22: Looked at the town, studied. Friday Luncheon at W. Unfortunately did not see Goethe's house.

Saturday, November 23: Rehearsal morning and afternoon. Radio orchestra pretty good. Some brass very good. Quick contact. (Hueber arrived Friday afternoon: in the evening rehearsed with him at Seligmann.) Two-hour rehearsal Saturday afternoon, in the morning from 9.30 to 1. After the rehearsal, rehearsed my violin and 'cello pieces, which will be performed there on November 27 in a concert by the IGNM. Went for a walk on Sunday morning At home in the afternoon. In the evening concert at 9.30.

> Programe: 1. Mozart: Divertimento in D major
> 2. Mahler: Kindertotenlieder, with Hueber
> 3. Mozart: G minor Symphony.

> 1. Better than in Vienna.
> 2. Very well achieved. Conducted it for the first time.
> 3. Very good.

Left early Monday morning for Cologne. Arrived Cologne midday. Met by Jalovec, evening at a concert (unhappy impression). Tuesday with Jal. in town. After noon at the cinema – Wednesday evening at the opera, then at Ph. Jarnach's*. Impressions of Cologne: wonderful

---

* Philipp Jarnach, composer and pupil of Busoni, whose "Doktor Faust" he completed. b. 1892.

town with much life! At home studied my Pieces op. 10.
Thurday, November 28 early: Left for London at a quarter
to seven. (Cologne: very happy at last to meet J.* again)
Via Aachen, Belgium to Ostend. Rain unhappy impression. From the train Brussels not a good impression. German form (architecture of town), here also
not particularly different. Ostend at midday, ate there.
Then on board ship. Crossing from three thirty to eight
o'clock. At first on deck. Sea very rough. Waves house
high. My state poor, but remained firm. Landed at eight.
Straight into the train. Arrived in London about 10.30.
Met by Clark*. Went with him to the Strand Palace Hotel
in town. Then to a party. Very tired. First rehearsal on
Friday morning. Orchestral Pieces (op. 10). Little comprehension from the orchestra. This quite good. After
rehearsal ate at home. Evening with Clark.
Saturday, November 30: Morning with Clark in the office.
Lunch. Afternoon second rehearsal of Orchestral Pieces,
Milhaud and part of Brahms Serenade. Then with Clark.
Sunday, December 1: Morning in town, afternoon at a
talking film, (much liked). Evening with Clark.
Monday, December 2: Final rehearsal, concert in the
evening: broadcast, but before an invited audience, in a
theatre (small, unpleasant).

Programe: 1. Milhaud: Les Printemps
               2. Orchesterstücke op. 10.
               3. Brahms: Serenade in A major, op. 16

* Jalovec.
* see note p. 56.

My pieces well achieved, more or less as in Zurich. But better there. Brahms played too dry. Milhaud also not very good. Played my pieces again at end of programme. Afterwards at a party. Brief. Then a restaurant.
Tuesday, December 3: Left early. Crossing to Ostend calm this time. Slept a lot. Left there at 4. Cologne about 1 o'clock. Saw Jalovec and wife again at station.
Wednesday, December 4: Arrived in Vienna Westbahnhof at 9.30 p.m. Minna and Peter and Christi at the station. Happy feeling. Incredibly happy impression on entering the house. Not much charmed by London. Tremendous traffic. But the whole atmosphere not sympathetic. Also applies to Cl. and the Orchestra. Social events insufferable. Could hardly wait to travel back. Rather disappointed. Impressions of sea, crossing coast: depressing. Fog, darkness, longing for the mountains and their climate, blue skies, clear air. Generally felt physically well. Weather in London *good*. Herewith end of the journey: was away from 15th November until the evening of 4th December (20 days)."

The years of 1929 and 1930 appear to have brought Webern increasing opportunities for concerts and teaching; these years might thus be regarded as the beginning of a climactic period which was to end in 1934, before it could really begin to develop. On 18th December, 1929, Webern travelled to Berlin to conduct his Passacaglia – an invitation that was probably due to the initiative of Schoenberg, with whom Webern stayed. 1929 also ended well with the successful first performance of his Symphony (op. 21) on 18th December in Philadelphia.

In 1930 the Austrian radio (RAVAG) named Webern, the conductor of the Workers' Symphony Concerts and the Workers' Choir, as its adviser on all questions concerning modern music. The compositorial results of the year were the well-known Quartet for clarinet, violin, tenor saxophone and piano (op. 22) in two movements, which Webern dedicated to his friend Adolf Loos, the outstanding architect, on his 60th birthday. As hitherto, his home and family remained the focal point for Webern, who had always tended to live a secluded life.

His activities as conductor of the Workers' Symphony Concerts and the radio concerts kept him busy throughout 1931; it was during the same year that the first concert dedicated exclusively to his works took place in the small Musikverein-Saal, with the participation of his old friends and colleagues, Kolisch, Steuermann and other experts in modern music. This helped to affirm his position as a composer in Vienna. As if to reaffirm and underline this tendency the Vienna City Council awarded Webern, for the second time, in the spring of 1932 the music prize of the City of Vienna of 3000 Schillings – a sum which naturally helped his family budget. Some long-needed purchases, e.g. a typewriter, were made with it. Unfortunately, a large part of the prize money went on moving house, since Webern suddenly imagined it necessary to live within the city, so as to be within more easy reach of his pupils and various centres important to him. He gave up his attractive apartment in Mödling and moved into Vienna, if only for a brief spell (the trouble and expense of the move were hardly worth it), since on 8th August, 1932, he noted in his diary "rented apartment Im Auholz 8". It seems to show that Webern was unable to stand the atmosphere of the large city any longer. The apartment "Im Auholz 8", on the edge of the woods within the commune of Maria Enzersdorf, near the so-called Kalenderberg, not far from Mödling, offered several advantages. Above all a garden which Webern was able to cultivate himself, in which he was able to plant and grow flowers to his heart's content, something that made him very happy, as he repeatedly told and wrote to his friends. But before he could move to his beautiful new villa – a detached, one-family residence which was to be his final home – several important works had to be completed. At the beginning of April (5th and 7th) 1932, Webern had been invited to conduct at the Barcelona International Music Festival – an invitation probably arranged by Schoenberg, who had lived for some time near Barcelona, and to which Webern looked forward. His happy hopes seem to have been fulfilled, since he wrote a postcard to Berg from Barcelona on 9th April.

"Dearest Alban, Chronologically; Schoenberg's concerts glorious, particularly "Pelleas" which I've never heard like this before. Orchestra outstanding. The best I've ever conducted. And my concert – I think – went well. I am highly satisfied. All else when we meet. Now holidays with Schoenberg. He lives in incredibly beautiful surroundings. – Home Tuesday via Paris. Here is real southern vegetation. The town is very beautiful and agreeable, but not really hot. Greetings to you and to your family, from Your Webern".

After his return from Barcelona Webern had to make haste to leave again for his second concert engagement in London during the first half of May. He did not seem displeased, since he could leave the Viennese atmosphere behind – an atmosphere which, probably for political reasons, had become increasingly unpleasant. In London he appears to have left a good impression as a conductor, since the BBC repeatedly invited him in this capacity. This time it was a case of two concerts – Schubert, Johann Strauss, Schoenberg, Webern – which he conducted successfully.

Work was awaiting him when he returned to Vienna on May 13th. A few days later the Universal-Edition commissioned Webern to orchestrate Schubert's newly discovered "Deutsche Tänze", a task the composer gladly undertook (with all his subtle chamber music talents); he was able to hand over the finished score to the publishers on June 17th.

Unfortunately Webern's diary entries end here. Only once more was he to note anything in the slim silk-bound volume (in the possession of his second daughter Maria Halbich): a short entry: "6. V. 1939: received printed score of my string quartet op. 28".

After the composer's death his widow entered the dates of the death of his son Peter and that of Webern himself in the little volume.

Chronologically it should be noted that in the spring of 1933 Webern undertook another – his third – concert

engagement in London. In a letter which he wrote to
Hildegard Jone on 3rd May, 1933, after his return, he
referred to the programme and his activities.

"Dear Friends, I have only been back from London a
few days. Though it was strenuous – I had to undertake
33 hours of orchestral rehearsal and two concerts in six
days – it was nevertheless very satisfying. Some things
gave me great pleasure: e.g. Mahler's Fourth. How I
wished that you could have listened . . . .".

During this period Webern led a quiet retired life
which accorded with his own desires. In Austria the
political climate was becoming unpleasant. Quite apart
from the conflict between the important Christian Social
party and the workers' parties, leading to clashes under
the surface, the National Socialist party was becoming
increasingly and disagreeably noticeable, as a result of
centrally directed provocations and clashes. Only a short
while before, as a result of a combination of various unhappy circumstances, it had come to power in Germany;
the Austrian-born Adolf Hitler had been designated
German Chancellor by the weak Hindenburg. Already in
1933 German Nazi propaganda, supported by the youth
of various classes, attempted to subvert Austria, and to
whip up and terrorise the Austrian people. A man of
Webern's outlook, who had been put on the Nazi-
German "black list" as a "cultural Bolshevik" obviously
suffered greatly. Probably his diary note referred to
these conditions: "Everything is becoming increasingly horrible; what is being done to me here day by
day is already hardly bearable. Perhaps salvation

from these terrible conditions in Vienna will come
for me."

The civil war in Austria in February 1934, the political
changes, the labour unrest, the clearly right-wing,
almost fascist attitude of the Austrian government, led
to the forced dissolution of the Austrian social democratic
party, and thus to the collapse of Webern's professional
existence (the Workers' Symphony Concerts, the Workers' Chorus, etc.). It was a hard blow for a man so politically uncommitted, who was merely emotionally attached
to a social philosophy. In spite of these events Webern
completely succeeded in isolating himself spiritually in
his home in Mödling, and was even able to compose: in
1933–34 he wrote his first compositions on texts by
Hildegard Jone – the songs Viae Inviae (op. 23), and in
1934 his Concerto for 9 instruments (op. 24).

To make good the loss of earnings from the Workers'
Symphony Concerts and the Workers' Choir, since he
now probably had no other fixed income than the pay-
ments from the Universal publishing house, Webern was
compelled to give more private lessons. But even this
became increasingly difficult; few wished to take lessons
with a man regarded as a "cultural Bolshevik" or "lackey
of the Jews" in a country with a fascist regime which, in
the early thirties, was increasingly looking towards Nazi
Germany. Thus Webern lectured on modern music in
various private houses in Vienna, where the "old guard"
of modern music around Schoenberg met almost illicitly.
(The lecture series "The Path to the New Music" and
"The Path to Music with Twelve Notes" which Webern

gave within this framework, has since been published by Universal Edition based on the shorthand notes of Dr. Rudolf Ploderer). To provide Webern with a small honorarium, the Austrian radio appointed him to a kind of "listening service", which in fact his daughters undertook.

These then were the new circumstances and changes, which Webern experienced between 1934 and 1938. He was saved by his house in Mödling-Maria Enzersdorf, with its garden to which he devoted much time and effort. And time he now had, more than he wished for.

In spite of the pressure of circumstances new works were written, works based on texts by Hildegard Jone, whose philosophy and language attracted Webern. Thus he wrote the Lieder (op. 25) (1935); the choral cantata Das Augenlicht (op. 26) (1935); and the Piano Variations (op. 27) (1936); the latter being something of a compendium of Webern's technique as a composer. During this period of almost complete retirement Webern twice travelled abroad as a conductor. In April 1935 – the year when a malignant disease suddenly took his dearest friend Alban Berg – the BBC again invited him to conduct a concert which was to contain some of Webern's own works; among them was the first performance of Bach's Ricercare for six voices from the Musical Offering, which Webern had recently orchestrated. And in 1936 Dr. Werner Reinhart, a generous patron who had done much to further modern music, invited Webern to give a concert of modern music in Winterthur. Apart from these few small excursions to countries not yet intimidated by fascism Webern retired increasingly to Mödling, there to teach the few pupils that remained. Time thus passed, until in March 1938 national socialism established itself in Austria also. Webern had no taste for political slogans, and as a quiet, sensitive and introverted man, he loathed noisy demonstrations and manifestations. He did not warm towards antisemitism which, in view of his admiration for Mahler, Schoenberg and his old teacher Guido Adler, was hardly surprising. It was therefore natural that Webern found nothing positive in the philosophy of national socialism or in the whole complex of fascism, and as a result isolated himself from both national socialism and the world it encompassed. For the rest the ineluctable drive of national socialism towards war kept Webern, a convinced pacifist, as far away as possible from the Nazi ideology.

For a time nothing changed his mode of life. He continued to live in the same reserved manner after 1938 as that which had marked his life from 1934 onwards. He retired completely to his villa in Mödling, and only his closest intimates saw him there. And he managed to work in spite of difficulties, in the knowledge that soon it would no longer be possible either to print or to perform his works within the German-speaking world.

In this atmosphere the String Quartet (op. 28) was completed in 1938; in 1939 the first cantata (to words of Hildegard Jone); in 1940 the Variations for Orchestra, (op. 30). From then on the Universal-Edition publishing house, which in the meantime had passed into German hands (few of its original members had remained in their posts) employed Webern as a reader and proof reader. He even had to arrange piano scores at that time for the publishing house, as a letter of 20th October, 1939 shows. Nevertheless, this type of work did not save him from the "total call-up", which compelled him to train in an anti-aircraft barracks, where he temporarily lived, as an air raid warden. This in spite of the fact that, on 3rd December, 1943, he was to celebrate his 60th birthday, quietly and among only a few of his closest friends. In 1943 Webern travelled abroad for the last time, to Basle (March 1943) for the first performance of his Orchestral Variations. He also finished his last complete work, the 2nd cantata to words of Hildegard Jone, later published as op. 31. In 1944 he began a work found after his death, sketches and designs for a chamber concerto which would have carried the opus number 32.

As the war progressed, moving towards its hopeless climax for Germany, Webern was increasingly overcome by a terrible anxiety about the future. In the spring of 1945 his only son Peter had been killed on the Yugoslav front, between Zagreb and Lubljana, in a low level air attack. Webern could not get over the tragic loss of his thirty-year old son, and being gripped by a panic that lacked all sense, he decided during Easter 1945 to leave Mödling on foot (trains for civilians no longer ran in Austria at this stage), in an attempt to reach the Salzburg area. There he hoped to stay near his children, who had in the meantime found shelter at Zell-am-See, for the remaining part of the war.

The description of the last days of Anton Webern

stems in the main from an account given by his second
daughter, Maria Halbich. Frau Halbich was by her
father's side both during the final unhappy period and
at is tragic end; her account should rightly be regarded
as valid. Perhaps this description will help to correct the
wrong impressions of Webern's last hours which have
continued to find currency.

Besides his overwhelming personal anxiety regarding
the final phases of the war, Webern in the spring of 1945
was probably filled with longing for his daughters, who
had repeatedly invited him to come to the Salzburg area.
The youngest daughter Christine and the second daughter Maria had settled in 1944 in Mittersill, on the Krimm-
ler railway line. And so, driven by fear and by longing
for his children, Webern decided to start on the road to
Mittersill on Easter Saturday 1945. Since the railways
were functioning badly throughout Austria, Webern and
his wife left Mödling on foot, equipped only with knap-
sacks and the most important of their belongings. But
at a small station near Rekawinkel the couple were, quite
unexpectedly, able to catch a train, and, after some
further difficulties, reached Mittersill. In Zell-am-See
the Weberns met their eldest daughter Amalia, who was
also trying to reach Mittersill. At last the Webern
family – if it can still be called that after the war-
time death of the son – found itself together in Mittersill, with the exception of the sons-in-law, who were
away in the forces. The son-in-law Mattl, the husband
of Christine, the youngest, arrived, however, a few
days later. There they intended to await the end

of the war. Mittersill lay alongside the main western route of retreat of the German army, and defeated and isolated groups of German troops continuously marched through the village.

With the exception of compulsory billeting, the Webern family suffered little. Even the Americans hoped to billet themselves on the Webern household, but were dissuaded from doing so by the large number of children from the different families. Their home was a small one, belonging to the son-in-law Halbich (or rather to his parents), and was probably rather a tight fit for thirteen people (7 children and 6 adults), although just adequate in the circumstances. Round about Whitsuntide, the son-in-law Günther Waller returned to Mittersill on foot from the Czechoslovak frontier, where he had held his last military position. In the course of the summer, probably in August, he was equally successful in venturing through the American-Russian occupation frontier line near Ems to reach Vienna. Visiting "Im Auholz" in Mödling-Maria Enzersdorf, where the Wallers also had an apartment, he found that the Russians and "dear neighbours" had behaved like vandals in Webern's house, and in his own apartment. Webern's possessions had been partly destroyed, had disappeared or been looted. His valuable library containing many unique special and first editions had been largely destroyed, some of the books had been stolen, others stuffed in bundles in the cellar or the canal. Irreplaceable manuscripts and letters shared the fate of the library. It was due to the initiative of his son Peter's widow that at least some of the contents of the house were saved.

For the greater part, the furniture had been smashed or removed; of the more valuable contents (silver, china, pictures, etc.) only a part could be found. All the articles had been carefully packed and listed by the Weberns and left in a summer house in the garden, where they fell prey to looters.

Webern's daughters did not tell their father of the destruction of his home in Mödling, and so he knew nothing of it before he died.

Though rather crowded, but basically in conditions which were neither unhappy nor unbearable, the Webern family spent this summer of 1945 in Mittersill.

On the evening of September 15th Webern went to visit his son-in-law Mattl, who in the meantime had moved to another house about fifteen minutes away. Mattl, who was then frequently engaged in black market deals, had been successful in finding a cigar, which Webern smoked with great pleasure. At the time such a cigar was a real rarity, available only by chance from the Americans. That evening Webern dined with his son-in-law Mattl and his family, who also lived in rather crowded conditions.

After supper the members of the family were sitting together with the small children in one room, when some Americans arrived to "do business with Mattl", as they put it, groceries and such like. While Mattl went into the kitchen with the American soldiers, Webern lit his precious cigar. Thinking of the sleeping children, he did not wish to fill the room with cigar smoke, and so went outside. It was about 9 p.m. and already rather dark.

During this period there was a limited curfew for the civilian population: no one was supposed to be outside after 8 p.m.

The Americans had wished to set a trap for Mattl, who to their annoyance was engaged in forbidden currency transactions, and so had failed to inform him of the recently imposed curfew regulations. That anyone else could be temporarily present in the Mattl house had not occurred to them. Apparently, Mattl was about to be arrested for his black market activities, and other American soldiers surrounded the house. Anton Webern, who quite innocently had stepped outside with his lighted cigar, became the unhappy victim of an over-eager U.S. soldier who, without further warning, shot three times at the man outside the house. All three shots hit Webern (two in the abdomen, one in the lung); with ebbing strength he was able to return to the house with the words "I have been hit; it's over". In the presence of his wife and of the small children he died shortly afterwards.*

One immediate result of this event was the arrest of Mattl, and shortly after of his wife Christine. In the meantime Webern's wife was confined to the house. His body was at once confiscated by the U.S. troops and taken away. Mattl was eventually tried for illegal currency dealings and imprisoned for a year. After two days Mattl's wife was released. A few days later Webern's

---

* For further details see Hans Moldenhauer, The Death of Anton Webern, Vision Press, London and Philosophical Library, New York.

widow succeeded in having his body returned to her for burial, which took place at the Mittersill cemetery. There Webern's grave remains.

Naturally, the shooting had its consequences shortly afterwards before a U.S. military court. Regrettably, Webern's widow was compelled to testify. The unhappy marksman, described as a tall, strong chap, entered a plea of "having had to act in self-defence", since Webern "had attacked him with an iron bar". The soldier showed an injury on his leg, which must have been caused some time before, since it had almost completely healed. He said that Webern had caused it with that iron bar. But this version of the tragic account can only be described as fantastic and grotesque. As demonstrated by the whole of his past life, Webern was a retiring, shy being, disliking every form of rough dealing or force. In addition, during this period – September 1945 – he was in very poor health: for the greater part of the summer he had suffered from a form of dysentery that had kept him in bed and had left him enfeebled to the point of becoming extremely thin. The fateful visit to his son-in-law Mattl was the first time in many weeks that Webern had left his own apartment in the evening. It is difficult to accept that a man of his character and ethics – greatly weakened after a lengthy illness – should have fought with an armed American soldier, particularly with a big, strong, young and healthy man.

After the military court hearing the Americans at once moved the battalion that had been stationed in Mittersill to another place. The request of Webern's widow for a pension and for damages was refused by the American court on the grounds that her husband had been killed in self-defence.

That a man devoted to the ideals of reflection, to a quiet retired existence, an artist totally opposed to undesirable publicity, should have found his end in this manner is indeed tragic. The noisy publicity after his death was long to disturb the peace of the musician and of his music – just as the younger generation today wrongly write the name of Webern on its battle flags to justify its own works. Wrongly, for they are far removed from Webern's actual thought. He was a true musician, who always bore in mind the ideals of comprehensible and communicable artistic expression, whether the results of his works realised these ideals or not.

CRITICAL CATALOGUE OF WORKS

The note–row tables appended to the discussion of the later works, i. e. the explanation of the twelve-note rows used for individual compositions, were those written in Webern's own hand and found among his effects.

1. *Piano Quintet (for 2 violins, viola, 'cello and piano).*

Webern composed the Piano Quintet in 1907 during his lessons with Schoenberg, who believed in asking his pupils to undertake composition exercises based on artistic expression and creative need. Webern thus completed this task, apparently wishing to write a sonata movement in C major for this particular chamber combination. It is impossible to ascertain whether he intended to add other movements to it. Dr. Josef Polnauer, who wrote an essay on Webern's early piano quintet, states that Webern composed the piece in memory of his mother, who had died in 1906. The work, in one movement, is written in a pure C major, making hardly any concessions to a more extended tonality.

Under Schoenberg's auspices the piano quintet was performed in a private house in Vienna before invited guests. No other public performances are known to have

taken place during Webern's life. It is believed that in
his later years Webern thought of rewriting the piano
quintet and of publishing it, but he did not realise his
intention. After 1945 an American publisher (Bomart)
printed the quintet, with the permission of Webern's
heirs, in facsimile form. Since then the piece has been
repeatedly performed in public, thus permitting an insight
into Webern's earliest style of composition.

2. The *Passacaglia* op. 1, Webern's "apprentice piece"
from the period spent with Schoenberg, was composed in 1908, the last work stemming directly from
Schoenberg's teaching. In it, particularly in the mastery
of the traditional means of composition, Webern demonstrated his full maturity. In this pure "Passacaglia", with
changing variations on a traditional eight-bar ostinato
bass theme, he uses the widened tonality employed
by Schoenberg in his earlier works. From the traditional
point of view, it is a work easy to comprehend. As a
result, and particularly in more recent times, it has been
increasingly performed internationally.

3. *"Entflieht auf leichten Kaehnen"*
(Poem by Stefan George) op. 2.

Double canon in four parts for mixed chorus a cap-
pella, composed in 1908 and included as opus 2 in
Webern's works. Its melodic substance is completely
tonal, with some essential admixture of chromatic alteration; the harmony, which has a remarkable precision
and cleanliness in its contrapuntal structure, is analogous.

This work was performed for the first time in 1927 – i.e.
nineteen years after its composition – by the amateur
choral society of the little town of Fuerstenfeld in Styria,
and soon after, in the same year, in Vienna by the Stutt-
gart Madrigal Society.

   4. *Five Lieder from "Der siebente Ring" by Stefan
      George for voice and piano, Op. 3.*

      1) "Dies ist ein Lied für dich allein"
      2) "Im Windesweben ..."
      3) "An Baches ranft ..."
      4) "Im Morgentaun trittst du hervor ..."
      5) "Kahl reckt der Baum im Winterdunst ..."

Here Webern demonstrates convincingly his detachment from the traditional song form of the late romantic
and post-romantic era, and from the traditional and
formal laws of tonal music. The melodic lines are
held together through motivic working, without any
side glances at traditional thematic working. In the
same way the departure from tonality in the musical
language, the mastering of the "musical style of freedom" is already superficially documented by the
abandonment of all key signatures. The individual songs
are aphoristically brief. Several of those collected here
date from the period of study with Schoenberg. For this
reason alone the theory of some "serial" dogmatists and
theoreticians that these songs particularly (and those of
opus 4) demonstrate the existence of a conscious "fight
in advance" for serial theories can hardly be justified.

5. Five Lieder on texts by Stefan George, Op. 4.

Within a style that is closely related to the Lieder
op. 3, the highly singable melody for voice is accompanied by a lucid, transparent piano part. It is kept
within a "free atonality", almost without final cadential
effects. The motivic connection of the total material of
each song is less apparent than the atmospheric connection, which is due more to a continuing stress on the text
(without any trace of pictorialism) than to an actual
"absolute" musical construction. These songs, composed
in 1908 and 1909, appear firmer, clearer and more
mature in style and in their direct lyrical expression than the Lieder op. 3 (1907/1908): however they are
sharply different from Schoenberg's early works, since
they have no connection with tradition. The piano part
is strictly pianistic, and is based more on chords than on
a linear structure.

The songs, composed on texts by Stefan George – at
this time the mood and expression of this poet appear to
have been close to Webern – have the following titles:

1. Eingang ("Welt der Gestalten...") (Ruhevoll,
   $7/4$)

2. "Noch zwingt mich Treue, über dir zu wachen..."
   (Bewegt, $3/4$)

3. "Ja, Heil und Dank dir..." (Sehr langsam, $4/4$)

4. "So ich traurig bin..." (Sehr fliessend und zart,
   $3/8$)

5. "Ihr tratet zu dem Herde..." (Langsam, $2/4$)

6. *Five Movements for String Quartet, Op. 5.*

These five pieces for string quartet, containing many unusual effects (all kinds of pizzicato, sul ponticello, sul tasto, harmonics of all sorts, etc.), are particularly interesting for Webern's development, since here he turns in his manner of writing to aphoristic brevity (a legacy of Schoenberg's piano pieces op. 19), and to great motivic concentration. They were to become typical of Webern's musical expression; he was to develop it further in this way. In this work Webern demonstrated for the first time his departure from traditional thematic composition and form, from construction dictated by themes. For this reason these short pieces, with their loosened rhythms and their completely free harmony – bound neither by note rows nor by tonal functions – and with their dynamics extended to extremes, must be regarded as one of the earliest valid documents of radical expressionism.

The pieces, written as string quartet movements, were composed in Vienna in 1909 with the title "Fünf Sätze für Streichquartett". In 1930 Webern himself rewrote them for string orchestra, keeping closely to their structural substance.

When Webern heard the "Five Movements for String Quartet" in 1934 at a concert, he wrote to Hildegard Jone: "I am happy that you and Pepo were so impressed by my quartet. It is now a quarter of a century since I wrote it. But since until recently there have been controversies about it, I do not really feel that it is so long ago. As for myself, it is only now that I can more clearly explain what I then did. And yet it seems to me as if the other day I heard the same as I did twenty-five years ago."

7. *Six Pieces for Orchestra, Op. 6.*

The orchestral pieces op. 6 in their first form of 1909 have these titles:

1. Etwas bewegte Achtel
2. Bewegt
3. Zart bewegt
4. Langsam, Marcia funebre
5. Zart bewegt.

These orchestral pieces show Webern's orchestral ideal of sound for the first time – a sound as transparent as possible, almost like chamber music, which once and for all left behind Wagnerian and post-Wagnerian orchestral writing, with its many doublings and massive middle parts. But in 1909, when Webern had just succeeded in shaking off tonal fetters, there was no question of a twelve-note ordering of the sound material. For the composer it remained a question of achieving essentially concentrated orchestral writing, a compressed expression in a manner reminiscent of "musical shorthand". As a result the pieces are brief, the longest no more than forty bars. The six orchestral pieces, which Webern re-orchestrated in 1932, and re-arranged in order to achieve a still greater "chamber music transparency", show the discovery of new melodic lines, new tonal combinations, and also new tone colours derived from the essence of the writing (and with it the discovery of the concept of

"tone colour" as a new dimension of musical expression).
This was more than decoration or addition.*

8. *Four Pieces for Violin and Piano, Op. 7.*

These highly concentrated pieces, written in 1910,
already demonstrate the composer's conscious attempts
to express every musical thought in the briefest possible
form. They are, so to speak, the basis, as well as the point
of departure, for those works of the middle period –
without being built on the concept of a twelve-note
structure – that finally break with the old tonal connections; they also finally do away with traditional
thematic form. In their place motivic working appears,
with extremely brief motifs of only a few notes, sometimes only highly expressive, isolated single notes acting
as motifs. Among others, the tonal language of the
Orchestral Pieces op. 10 and the 'Cello Pieces op. 11 are
developed from the Violin Pieces. They are as follows:

> 1st Piece: (9 Bars) Sehr langsam (♪ = ca. 50)
> 2nd Piece: (24 Bars) Rasch (♩ = 112)
> 3rd Piece: (14 Bars) Sehr langsam (♪ = ca. 60)
> 4th Piece: (15 Bars) Bewegt (♩ = ca. 84)

Webern several times played the piano part of these
pieces: Arnold Rosé or Rudolf Kolisch interpreted the
violin part.

---

* These pieces were first performed on 31st March, 1913, at a
concert in Vienna conducted by Schoenberg, together with Schoenberg's First Chamber Symphony and Berg's Altenberglieder, op. 4.
The music caused a riot in the audience.

9. *Two Songs on Texts of Rainer Maria Rilke, Op. 8.*

for voice, clarinet (also bass clarinet), horn, trumpet, celesta, harp, solo violin, solo viola, solo 'cello.

The two Rilke songs were written in 1910. They manifest in the first place sounds which arise from the special positioning of dissonant intervals which, nevertheless, as originally shown in the string quartet pieces op. 5, represent nothing more than colour values. On close inspection of this relatively early score, it becomes clear that the typical "Webern sound" remained the same throughout the whole period of the composer's further development. And this was so whether Webern used a strictly twelve-note construction or sounds deriving from a free and doctrinally unconnected atonality. During his middle period the rhythmic picture – whether twelve-note or not – remained basically the same. Special care was lavished on the development of the voice part, which declaims the poems well and clearly but is not afraid to go as far as the frontiers of the abstract, which, indeed, accords with Rilke's texts.

Opus 8 consists of two Rilke poems; No. 1, "Du, der ich's nicht sage, dass ich bei Nacht weinend liege..." (Langsam $\downarrow$ = ca. 50, 14 bars) and no. 2 "Du machst mich allein, dich einzig kann ich vertauschen..." (Sehr langsam, $\downarrow$. = 44, 18 bars). The length of performance of these two very difficult songs together is about five minutes.

10. *Six Bagatelles for String Quartet, Op. 9.*

These are six very brief aphoristic pieces in Webern's characteristic manner, which in their substance are a reworking and intensification of the manner of the quartet pieces op. 5. They were composed in 1913, and were heard for the first time at the Donau-Eschingen Music Festival, where the Hindemith Quartet performed them in the summer of 1919. In the printed version (Universal-Edition) Arnold Schoenberg wrote his now famous foreword that wonderingly appreciates Webern's new tendencies, which were increasingly to diverge from that of his master. He wrote "Though the brevity of these pieces is a persuasive advocate for them, on the other hand that very brevity itself needs an advocate. Consider what moderation is required to express oneself so briefly. Each glance can be extended into a poem, each sigh into a novel. But to express a novel in a single gesture, a joy in a single indrawn breath, such concentration can only be found where self-pity is absent. These pieces will only be understood by those who believe that through sound something that can only be expressed through sound can be said. They stand up as much or as little to criticism as this or any belief.

"If faith can move mountains, then lack of faith cannot allow them to exist. Against such impotence belief is impotent. Does the musician now know how to play these pieces, the listener how to accept them? Can believing players and listeners fail to be persuaded? But what shall one do with the heathen? The fire and the sword can

keep them quiet: but only the believers need to be
restrained. May this silence sound for them."

11. *Five Pieces for Orchestra, Op. 10.*

The orchestral pieces op. 10 were written in Vienna in
1913. They represent a heightened sound image that – in
an almost impressionist manner – is dedicated to the re-
presentation of impressions of the countryside, specially
the sound of faraway herd bells, a touch showing
Webern's love of mountain life. Above all, these five
pieces show his detachment from any "building-up" com-
positional technique; they are short throughout.

1. Sehr ruhig und zart (12 Bars) ($\downarrow$ = ca. 50)
2. Lebhaft und zart bewegt (14 Bars) ($\downarrow$ = ca. 100)
3. Sehr langsam und aeusserst ruhig (11 Bars)
   ($\downarrow$ = ca. 40)

4. Fliessend, aeusserst zart (6 Bars) ($\downarrow$ = ca. 60)
5. Sehr fliessend (33 Bars) ($\downarrow$ = ca. 152)

There is no question here of a "technical structure",
hardly of definite motifs. In their place – in this almost
purely athematic succession of short pieces – changing
tone-colours and their construction play a large role. The
birth of the idea of "melody of tone-colour" appears as
a result, the concept of the division of a melodic structure
into groups of a few notes constantly changing in their
instrumental colour. On these orchestral pieces the essays
of Mersmann and Wiesengrund-Adorno are important,
instructive and characteristic. (See pp. 166, 173).

12. *Three Little Pieces for Violoncello and Piano, Op. 11.*

These pieces were composed in Vienna in 1914. They represent the extreme final point of Webern's concentrated brevity of musical expression. Compared with these 'cello pieces the strongly compressed Violin Pieces op. 7 might be called prodigal. Schoenberg's foreword to the Bagatelles for string quartet op. 9 may be regarded as particularly valid for these pieces: "... To express a novel in a single gesture, a joy in a single indrawn breath, such concentration can only be found where self-pity is absent". The forerunners of this concentrated brevity, within which a single subtly expressed note can replace a whole phrase, are found not only in the Violin Pieces op. 7, but also in some parts of the Orchestral Pieces op. 10. "These pieces will only be understood by those who believe that through sound something that can only be expressed through sound can be said."

Three printed pages are all that are needed for these pieces, which only last a few minutes. The 'cello produces remarkable sound-effects, each note is to be produced in a different way: with mute, without mute, harmonic sul ponticello, pizzicato, arco, sul tasto ...

The indications of the three pieces are:

1.) Maessig (9 Bars) (♪ = ca. 58)
2.) Sehr bewegt (13 Bars) (♩ = ca. 160)
3.) Äusserst ruhig (10 Bars) (♪ = ca. 50)

Webern himself was quite clear about the problems of these 'cello pieces, though basically they did not introduce

anything new or unusual for him. Thus he wrote to
Dr. Willi Reich on 20th October, 1939: "... For the rest,
the violin pieces are more suitable than the 'cello pieces.
Better not play those. Not because I do not think them
good. But they would only be misunderstood. The players
and the listeners can only understand them with difficulty."

13. *Four Songs for Voice and Piano, Op. 12.*

Compared to the Lieder op. 3 and 4, the Lieder op. 12
– composed between 1915 and 1917 – appear simpler,
easier to perform and to understand, more transparent
and more lapidary than the earlier works. They are a
continuation of a tendency, which had appeared more or
less clearly in the earlier works, to special compression
and concentration of the musical substance, a greater
density of the substance, musically as well as poetically.

Their titles

1. "Der Tag ist vergangen . . ." (Folksong, 1915).
   Sehr ruhig (♩ = ca. 60)
2. "Die geheimnisvolle Floete (Li-Tai-Po, translated
   by Bethge, 1917). Langsam (♩ = ca. 54)
3. "Schien mir's, als ich sah die Sonne . . ." (Strindberg, 1915). Ruhig fliessend (♩. = ca. 42)
4. "Gleich und gleich" (Goethe, 1915). Sehr fliessend
   (♩. = ca. 44)

14. *Four Songs for Voice and Orchestra, Op. 13.*

Orchestration: flute (also piccolo), clarinet in B flat
(also bass clarinet in B flat), horn in F, trumpet in B flat,

trombone, celesta, glockenspiel, harp, solo strings (one violin, one viola, one 'cello, one double bass).

The orchestra used by Webern for these songs, composed between 1917 and 1918, is really a chamber ensemble. The solo string instruments strongly stress the fact that it is here a matter of tender, solo effects; that the instrumental tone colour, not yet bound by twelve-note laws, but still moving within so-called free atonality, is to be with tender differentiation. The linear appearance of the Canons op. 16 has not yet been achieved; it is more a question of the instrumental colour (in all essentials of construction) of the Folk Texts op. 17. There the step from "free atonality" to strict twelve-note writing in Webern's vocal works is taken – as generally in all his works – without much friction. These four orchestral songs, ordered as follows, should be understood in this sense.

1. "Wiese im Park" (Karl Kraus). Sehr ruhig, ($\downarrow$ = ca. 60) Composed 1917.
2. "Der Einsame" (Wang-Seng-Yu, translated by Hans Bethge). Bewegt, ($\downarrow$ = ca. 84) Composed 1914.
3. "In der Fremde" (Li-Tai-Po, translated by Hans Bethge). Fliessend, ($\downarrow$ = 56) Composed 1917.
4. "Ein Winterabend" (Georg Trakl). Sehr ruhig, ($\downarrow$ = 56) Composed 1918.

15. *Six Songs for High Voice, clarinet, bass clarinet, violin and 'cello, Op. 14.*

The whole of Webern's Opus 14 is based on poems of Georg Trakl, whose expressive poetical form was close to the musical language used here. Almost everything possible in the way of remarkable sounds within the framework of a still free atonality, as well as within a "planned" concept, is realised here. Without becoming mere illustration the musical expression follows the meaning of the text. The songs are in the following order:

1. "Die Sonne" – Ruhig fliessend, $\quad$ = ca. 72, composed in 1921: instrumentation, soprano, clarinet, violin, 'cello.

2. "Abendland I" – Sehr lebhaft, $\quad$ = ca. 120, composed in 1919: instrumentation, soprano, bass clarinet, violin, 'cello.

3. "Abendland 11" – Langsam, $\quad$ = 46, composed in 1919: instrumentation, soprano, clarinet, violin, 'cello.

4. "Abendland 111" – Langsam, $\quad$ = 48, composed in 1917: instrumentation, soprano, clarinet, bass clarinet, 'cello.

5. "Nachts" – Sehr lebhaft, $\quad$ = 104, composed in 1919: instrumentation, soprano, clarinet, bass clarinet, violin.

6. "Gesang einer gefangenen Amsel" – Sehr fliessend Achtel, $\quad$ = ca. 120, composed in 1919: instrumentation, soprano, clarinet, bass clarinet, violin, 'cello.

16. *Five Sacred Songs for soprano, flute, clarinet (also bass clarinet), trumpet, harp, violin (also viola), Op. 15.*

These songs for soprano and a carefully selected chamber ensemble belong to the long series of vocal works of Webern's middle creative period (op. 12–19 inclusive): they show the composer more as an artist pre-occupied by colour and less as a master of linear drawing. They are closely related to the Trakl songs op. 14 in content and style. A large and important step in his development, which was to become characteristic of his future works, took place between the songs op. 15 and the very linear Canons op. 16 which followed, his last "pre-twelve-note work" (1924).

The Five Sacred Songs op. 15 show colourful and sensitive musical ideas (the colour values of the dissonances and the large intervals in the vocal line show an expressive coloration. These intervals, because of their almost abstract heightening of the declamation of the text, may have found their inspiration in the Sprechstimme melody of *Pierrot Lunaire*): the texts are simple popular poems of the kind that always appealed to Webern, particularly during the middle period.

The order of the songs is as follows:

1. "Das Kreuz, das musst er tragen..." Getragen, ♩ = ca. 60. Composed 1921. Instrumentation: soprano, flute, bass clarinet, trumpet, viola, harp.

2. "Morgenlied", "Steht auf, ihr lieben Kinderlein..." from "Des Knaben Wunderhorn". Zart

bewegt, ♪ = 60. Composed 1922. Instrumenta-
tation: soprano, bass clarinet, trumpet, violin,
harp.

3. "In Gottes Namen aufsteh'n . . ." Gemaechlich,
♩ = ca. 66. Composed 1921. Instrumentation:
soprano, clarinet, trumpet, viola.

4. "Mein Weg geht jetzt vorueber . . ." Sehr ruhig,
♩ = ca. 48. Composed 1922. Instrumentation:
soprano, flute, clarinet.

5. "Fahr hin, o Seel', zu deinem Gott . . ." Fliessend,
♩ = ca. 60. Composed as a double canon in motu
contrario, in 1917. Instrumentation: soprano, flute,
clarinet, trumpet, violin, harp.

17. *Five Canons for soprano, clarinet and bass clarinet, Op. 16,* composed 1923–24, published in 1928 by the
Universal Edition. The first piece is set to the Easter Thursday graduale "Christus factus est" as a three-part movement of which one part is taken over by the voice and
appears in contrast to the two clarinets. The three purely
linear canonic voices are in inversion or parallel movement (at the interval of a major second).   Rasch, ♩ = ca.
88.

The second, quiet piece is in two parts, a canon between clarinet and voice in inversion, at the distance of
four crotchets. The text is an old folk song, something
like a lullaby of Mary for the infant Jesus ("Dormi, Jesu,
mater ridet").

The clarinet begins, the voice imitates. Ruhig, ♩ = ca.
72.

The third movement sets a hymn of the Good Friday liturgy "Crux fidelis, inter omnes arbor una nobilis" as a straight canon in three parts (at the eleventh and the augmented fourth). Langsam, ♩ = ca. 50, Molto espressivo.

The fourth piece again is presented as a canon in two parts for soprano and bass clarinet on a verse taken from the Psalms: "Asperges me, Domine, hyssopo, et mundabor..." The canon is at the augmented octave at a distance of two quavers. Sehr lebhaft, ♩ = ca. 112.

As a finale, the fifth movement again forms a canon in three parts with the bass beginning, the middle part imitating at the augmented octave, and the upper part imitating in contrary motion. The distance between the parts in each case is two quavers. The text used is also a popular sacred poem: "Crucem tuam adoramus. Domine..." Bewegt, ♩ = ca. 84. The melodic lines move here in widely spaced intervals of the highest expressiveness.

This last work of Webern's to keep within "free atonality", without a strict twelve-note row, is above all fascinating in its style; this represents the true link with the strict twelve-note row technique in the strictly polyphonic and linear parallelism of the voices, which are entirely aligned to the ecstatically rising declamation of the text. No customary or traditional "thematic" material can be found here, but a convinced synthesis of a dynamic, motoristic and polyphonic kind. The music impresses by its complete concentration and brevity; but according to my view, this impression is secondary to its beautiful organic form and the expression of the melodic lines in all the canonic parts. The whole substance is limited to the essential polyphonic structure: there is no single part which merely fills out or colours the sound.

While composing these canons Webern wrote to Alban Berg on 23rd August, 1923: "... Even though I never let go for a moment (much begun, several repeatedly, much dropped.), I may say: three of the Latin lieder now exist. Perhaps this is the end of them. Now I should like to work at something different. These three songs are canons. The first one for voice and clarinet' (canon in the inversion); the second a straight three-part canon (voice, clarinet, bass clarinet); the third a two-part straight canon (voice and bass clarinet). In sound clearly differentiated. The first a kind of lullaby, (textually) of Mary; the second an Antiphon (song, prayer) to the crucifix. The third an invocation (holy water). The whole, I believe, in form and expression is musically well-rounded. Perhaps I shall leave it at these three."

Eventually Webern changed his mind, to complete the work in five movements: beginning, middle and end in three parts, each separated by one in two parts.

18. *Three Folk Texts for soprano, clarinet, bass clarinet, violin (also viola), 'cello, Op. 17.*

These songs were written in 1924 and were publicly performed for the first time in Cologne in 1953. They come towards the end of a group of compositions for voice. Here, as in the previous work (the canons, op. 16) the composer attempts to channel into strict forms the forces he had previously freed from traditional laws. In this process Schoenberg's technique of "composition with twelve notes related only to one another" was to prove of decisive importance to Webern. The Folk Texts op. 17 is Webern's first work which – still in primitive form – is constructed within the twelve-note style and which creates from the basic twelve-note row all its musical manifestations (melody, harmony) and its basic substance. In its intimate, ecstatic expression and the almost sensual charm of its sounds this work is characteristic of the "surrealist" style of Webern's middle period. The texts of these three songs are anonymous folk poems entitled:

1. "Armer Sünder du . . ." Gemächlich (♩ = ca. 56).
2. "Liebste Jungfrau, wir sind dein . . ." Fliessend (♩ = ca. 96).
3. "Heiland, unsre Missetaten . . ." (in place of the violin the viola is used.) Langsam (♪ = ca. 56).

19. *Three Songs for soprano, E flat clarinet and guitar, Op. 18.*

Webern wrote these songs in the autumn of 1925; he dedicated them to Dr. Emil Hertzka, the director of the Universal Edition who had greatly encouraged him, on the occasion of the Jubilee of the publishing house. (On this occasion all its composers had agreed to dedicate a composition to Dr. Hertzka; the compositions were intended to be bound in a special volume and presented to the director. Webern composed one of these songs for this volume and later added two more which he also dedicated to his friendly sponsor.)

These three songs are among the earliest compositions in which he used the twelve-note system of composition. Here the composer proves his ability as well as his indepedence in handling the new techniques both in colour, and in a style that makes no concessions in its unusual instrumental combination. The three songs are settings of folk texts:

1. "Schatzerl mein, musst nicht traurig sein . . ." Sehr ruhig, ♩ = ca. 54. Very tenderly differentiated sounds well divided between the instruments – E flat clarinet, guitar.

2. "Erlösung" (Text from "Des Knaben Wunderhorn"). Sehr bewegt, ♩ = ca. 100. Technically very difficult for all performers. Large intervals in the melodic lines, etc.

3. "Ave regina coelorum . . ." Marianic Latin hymn. Langsam, ♪ = ca. 56. Rhythmically and melodically difficult for all.

Webern himself wrote to Alban Berg about these songs on 8th October, 1925: ". . . I have now completed the second of this song series, 'Erlösung' from 'Des Knaben Wunderhorn'; the third will be a Latin song (Song of Mary): 'Ave, regina coelorum' . . . The connection that exists for me between these three poems I'll tell you about one day when we meet. I am now working on the third. The 'twelve-note composition' has already become quite clear to me. Naturally, these songs are all composed in this style. And the work gives me pleasure

as rarely anything before has. I am longing to show you
how it has worked out."

20. *Two Songs for Mixed Chorus, accompanied by
    celesta, guitar, violin, clarinet and bass clarinet,
    Op. 19.*

Webern had the idea of using these two poems by
Goethe from the "Chinesisch-deutschen Jahres- und
Tageszeiten" – he was an ardent admirer of Goethe – in
1926, shortly after he had mastered Schoenberg's twelve-
note method. Thus, these choruses keep throughout to a
strict twelve-note row technique in their composition.
The colour and sound of the choral passages are astonishing, both of them supported by the peculiar sound-
character of the accompanying instruments. The accompanied choral writing here might be regarded as an early
study for the later choral works. Naturally, however, the
writing for chorus and orchestra has not yet the clarity
and the ease shown in the later cantatas or the "Augenlicht". The two choral songs, dedicated to Dr. David
Josef Bach, use the poems "Weiss wie Lilien, reine Ker-
zen" . . . and "Zieh'n die Schafe von der Wiese . . ." No. 1
is marked "Lebhaft, leicht und drei" (♩ = ca. 104); No. 2
is marked "Sehr gemächlich" (♩ = ca. 60).

21. *String Trio, Op. 20.*

Webern composed his String Trio in the summer of 1927 in Hafning in Styria. Besides the strict twelve-note writing and the abstract language of this work, which employs the most extreme sound effects of the strings, its form, in two movements, is remarkable. Webern first planned a third movement and began it, but wrote in his diary on 22nd July, 1927: "After much reflection a difficult decision: gave up work on the third movement of my String Trio, leaving it in two movements. Fair copy of these two".

The first movement – Sehr langsam – resembles a typical classical rondo slow movement; the second is built on the principle of a sonata movement (with a slow introduction) with the reprise as a definite variation of the themes – not an exact repetition.

The whole work, which was first performed by the Kolisch Ensemble in the small hall of the Vienna Musikverein on 16th January, 1928, lasts nine and a half minutes.

Op. 20

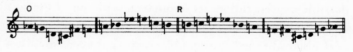

22. *Symphony, Op. 21.*

The Symphony op. 21 was completed at Mödling near Vienna in the summer of 1928. A relatively small instrumental ensemble is used (four wind instruments;

clarinet, bass clarinet, two horns; four solo strings: two violins, viola, 'cello; one harp) and in character it is more of a chamber music work than an orchestral one. The instrumentation is delicate and transparent, limited to essentials and does not attempt to achieve big effects – a characteristic also to be noted in Webern's earlier works.

The symphony consists of two contrasting movements. Webern began to sketch a third movement, but eventually decided – as with the Trio op. 20 and the Quartet op. 22 – to limit himself to two.

The first movement is built on canonic forms and their inversions and develops the phenomenon known as melody of tone colour – the splitting up of a melodic line into very small motifs and single notes. These then are put together in a mosaic form with a different sound colour and played by different instruments. The second movement consists of a theme and seven variations on the retrograde form of the series of the first movement: every note used can be deduced from serial, quasi–thematic basic material. Though this work shows the highest possible concentration, its sound as a critic put it "makes an extraordinarily nervous, unsettled impression; it seems as if all traditional musical elements had been atomised and reduced to a musical shorthand".

Op.21

23. *Quartet for clarinet, tenor saxophone, violin and piano, Op. 22.*

Webern wrote the Quartet op. 22 in 1930, and dedicated it to his friend, the famous architect Adolph Loos, on his sixtieth birthday. Webern had originally planned the work for clarinet, horn, violin and piano, and had even begun to do some sketches of this version. In his diary the composer noted on 10th December, 1930: "The sixtieth birthday of Adolph Loos. I dedicated my Quartet op. 22 to him. For it I had planned a third movement on which I worked in August and September. Finally decided to leave this work also in two movements". The first performance took place on 13th April, 1931, in the small hall of the Musikverein in Vienna, in the first concert ever dedicated entirely to Webern's music; Kolisch and Steuermann took part. The work is strictly twelve-note, ascetic in sound and effect, consisting of a brief first movement (sehr mässig, ♩. = ca. 36, 41 bars) and a longer second movement (sehr schwungvoll, ♩. = ca. 108, 192 bars). The extreme precision of its form and its compression were greatly admired by Alban Berg, who expressed himself to this effect in several letters to Webern.

Op.22

24. *Three Songs from "Viae Inviae" by Hildegard Jone, Op. 23.*

These three songs were written in 1934, partly immediately before and partly simultaneously with the "Concerto for Nine Instruments". In their concept the songs possibly show some links with the above-mentioned work. If the first songs with piano (op. 3 and 4) are compared with Webern's later songs with piano (as a kind of link there are the songs op. 12, 1915/17) – the increasing asceticism in the shaping of the melodic line is particularly striking (as are the those of the more economical piano part). They may be regarded as characteristic of Webern's developing musical expression. It should be noted in addition that the Songs op. 23 are worked in the strictest twelve-note technique, so that the material alone demands a certain asceticism and difficulty of sound, a way of expression natural to Webern from his middle period onwards.

The three Songs are based on these texts:

1. "Das dunkle Herz, das in sich lauscht..." (Getragen, $\downarrow$ = ca. 48)
2. "Es stuerzt aus Höhen Frische..." (Bewegt, $\downarrow$ = ca. 108)
3. "Herr Jesus mein..." (Langsam, $\downarrow$ = ca. 42)

Webern wrote to Hildegard Jone on 20th March, 1934, about the first song of this cycle: "In the meantime the third song has been completed. Since it embraces the words from 'Das dunkle Herz' to '...ich und du und alle' it has become rather long, and musically is really a kind of aria consisting of a slow section and from 'ich bin nicht mein' a faster one, which, nevertheless is marked 'ganz ruhig'. This second section is almost whispered. Perhaps you will be able, from this description, to gather more or less how I have understood the second section of your words in particular: after a large outburst to begin with, immediately complete calm, simplicity. I thought of the title as Three Songs from Viae Inviae."

The songs were given their first performance in Basle by the female singer, Grademann, at a concert dedicated to Webern by the local I.S.C.M. on 5th December, 1944; they had been published in 1936 by the Universal Edition.

Row of the Songs op. 23.

25. *Concerto for Nine Solo Instruments, Op. 24.* Instrumentation: flute, oboe, clarinet, horn, trumpet, trombone, violin, viola, piano.

If musicologists compare Webern's compositions to a "musical shorthand", this comparison is most apt with regard to this highly compressed piece. It employs twelve-note and serial construction in a particularly strict and consequential way, considering the compressed size of the

basic building materials. Here it is essential to concen-
trate on the brevity and the compression of the phrases,
the "pointillism" of the individual instruments, and the
large intervals in the melodic material, if the connection
of the amorphic-seeming tone structure is to be understood.

In its scheme this concerto returns to the three-move-
ment structure of the pre-classical concerto, though it is
projected, in a highly personal and individual manner,
onto a new plane. Its substance is governed by a three-
note basic phrase – a quarter of the twelve-note row
employed: the three movements of the work, each of
about 70 bars, are:

1. Etwas lebhaft ($\mathbf{J}$ = ca. 80)
2. Sehr langsam ($\mathbf{J}$ = ca. 40)
3. Sehr rasch ($\mathbf{J}$ = ca. 120)

Op. 24

26. *Three Songs for Voice and Piano on poems by
Hildegard Jone, Op. 25.*

The three songs op. 25 were written in 1934 at about
the same time as the concerto op. 24, and the song cycle
op. 23; closely related to the earlier songs, they use pure
twelve-note technique. Their form and their sound

picture, however, are even briefer, more ascetic, stricter, and limited to essential structural organisation. Generally, the works op. 23 and 25 should be regarded as linked to one another – partly because they were written at the same time, but also because their texts closely resemble one another. The Songs are as follows:

1. "Wie bin ich froh . . ." (Langsam, ♩ = ca. 60, Summer 1934)
2. "Des Herzens Purpurvogel . . ." (Fliessend, ♪ = ca. 112, October 1934)
3. "Sterne, ihr silbernen Bienen der Nacht . . ." (Sehr rasch, ♩ = ca. 96, October 1934)

27. *"Das Augenlicht" for Mixed Chorus and Orchestra, Op. 26.*

"Das Augenlicht" was written in the summer and autumn period of 1935. The score was completed in September 1935. Musically, "Das Augenlicht" could perhaps be regarded as a sort of preliminary study for the two last cantatas; in principle at least Webern may well have already been planning them at this stage. The poem, by Hildegard Jone, is set without any breaks. The basic tempo is "langsam". The orchestra of relatively large size (flute, oboe, alto saxophone, horn, trumpet, trombone, glockenspiel, cymbals, harp, celesta, mandoline, strings without double bass) divides the melodic events into small parts, mosaic-like fragments, so that each instrument usually has a motif of two, or at most three notes, sometimes only a single note, as in the "melody of tone colour" developed earlier by Webern. Thus the orchestral sound is thin and always transparent. This kind of orchestration avoids thicker and more massive sounds: double basses and bassoons are missing and the wind and percussion are used as soloists. The writing for chorus alternates between homophonic and polyphonic episodes. The polyphonic parts are intentionally transparent: in sections the writing is kept in two parts. Unison episodes are also inserted here and there, in place of polyphonic ones, between the homophonic sections.

The technical structure of the composition looks very strict in its conception; there are strict canonic imitations in recto and in inversion as well as definite motifs, etc. But everything is also treated with considerable freedom; the imitations, for example, do not always keep to the same intervals. In the first polyphonic episode, between two parts which are basically written in canon, the structure changes between canons in their straight form and in inversion. This is contrary to Webern's otherwise almost acrostic method of working. The impression prevails that more attention was paid to stressing the text, than to certain constructional tricks which, while Webern undoubtedly enjoyed them, he never permitted to become the substance of a work.

This knowledge appears to have been used in the structure of the row given in the illustration below. This is no "qualified pre-fabricated" row. It is in no way identical ,in its intervals with its ,retrograde; its first half also differs in its intervals from its second half and from the inversion of its second half. Also, there are no correspondences between the three or four-note groups. But the row permits the derivation of several different, characteristic interval steps, which are kept identical throughout the whole piece, and also allows a freer form of composition. The sounds arising from it are never hard or hurtful, but throughout show a soft colouring. The unusual intervals with which the choral melody is richly spiced are a part of this sound colour, as indeed was to be the case in the last cantatas.

28. *Variations for Piano, Op. 27.*

Webern completed this work in 1936, soon after the "Augenlicht" and the "Concerto for Nine Instruments", and before the String Quartet op. 28. In connection with it he wrote to Hildegard Jone on 18th July, 1936: "... I worked well, a part of my new work is ready. I told you that I was writing something for piano. What is complete is a variation movement. It will be a sort of "suite". With the "Variations" I hope to have realised something I have had in mind for years. Goethe once told Eckermann, when the latter greatly praised a new poem, that he had thought about it for forty years." The Piano Variations are in three movements: the first is in the form of a prelude, (sehr mässig) of 54 bars; a brief quasi-scherzo of 22 bars (sehr schnell); and the third (ruhig fliessend), which is the real variation movement. These piano variations are probably the most concentrated work of the later Webern, making no concessions whatsoever; they are often quoted by the exponents of serial* composition as showing Webern's so-called pioneering role in serial music. More detailed analyses of this work can be found in Jelinek (Anleitung zur Zwölfton-Komposition) and in the Webern volume of Die Reihe (No. 2, page 85), where Armin Klammer analyses the third movement of the work from a serial point of view.

Op.27

29. *String Quartet, Op. 28.*

When Webern began in 1937 to sketch a new String Quartet, a commission arrived from an American patron,

---

* ie, *total* serialisation of all elements.

Elizabeth Sprague Coolidge (to whom this work, as also
Schoenberg's third string quartet, is dedicated). On 23rd
December, 1937 he wrote to Hildegard Jone: "A very
pleasant commission has come from America. I have been
asked for the dedication of a string quartet, instead of, as
originally required, some other from of chamber music.
Thus everything is now nicely resolved, since my present
work is a string quartet. So I need not interrupt my labours,
am not pushed, and can finish at the right time without
any difficulty." The row on which this strict twelve-note
piece is based (see illustration below) has a very concentrated structure and permits different, very complicated relations. In its structure and style the work is
kept very much "splintered" in its external appearance,
making a very "doctrinaire" impression. The score
clearly demonstrates that it was written at roughly the
same time as the piano variations, op. 27 and the first
cantata, op. 29.

The String Quartet is divided into these movements.

1. Mässig (♩ = ca. 66)
2. Gemächlich (♩ = ca. 56)
3. Sehr fliessend (♪ = ca. 112)

30. *Cantata on texts by Hildegard Jone, Op. 29,* composed 1939.

The work is written for soprano solo, mixed chorus and orchestra (chamber music orchestration) and divided into three movements which together take less than ten minutes.

1. Chorus (getragen, 47 Bars) "Zündender Licht-blitz des Lebens . . ."
2. Soprano-Solo (leicht bewegt, 56 bars) "Kleiner Flügel Ahornsamen . . ."
3. Chorus and Soprano solo (ruhig, 73 bars) "Tönen die seligen Saiten . . ."

Here a twelve-note row technique is used which is pure, masterful and carefully arranged; it handles the material with complete virtuosity. While working on the Cantata No. 1, and immediately after its completion, Webern discussed the work several times – the best introduction to the work for the reader. Thus Webern wrote on 9th December, 1939 to his friend and pupil Dr. Willi Reich: ". . . The cantata (op. 29) is complete . . . in construction it is a double fugue in four parts. But the subject and counter-subject are related like antecedent and consequent, thus bringing into play the elements of the other (horizontal) method. It would be possible to speak of a scherzo or variations. Yet it is a strict fugue. For chorus, soprano solo and orchestra. I am now busy writing the full score."

To the author of the text, Frau Jone, Webern wrote on 2nd December, 1939: "I should like to tell you that the 'Chariten'* are complete. The piece gave me much work.

---

* the original title of the work; author's note.

In its construction it is a fugue in four parts, but to gain
freedom of movement within this form, so that there can
be no question of strain, that was not easy. As a result, it
turned out differently, a scherzo in form on the basis of
variations. Yet, still a fugue. Now I am busy with the
full score. This will still take much time: i.e. to achieve
a sound which has not hitherto come to my mind in such a
varied way. This cantata would be composed in this way.
I believe that the 'Chariten' will have to be the first piece,
for musical as well as for textual reasons. Do not the
'Kleiner Flügel' and 'Blitz und Donner' provide the
answer to the question of the 'Chariten' verse, dear
Hildegard? Do they not express what is meant by it, with
"sound", with "words", with "seal of the spectrum"?
Naturally the 'Chariten' are based on the same series of
twelve notes ('row') as the other two pieces. As I already
told you this row possesses the characteristic that the
second six notes in the intervals represent the retrograde
inversion of the first six, so that everything that happens
is related to a series of six notes. Always the same; whether it is the 'Seligen Saiten', the 'Anmut der Gnade', the
'Kleiner Flügel', the 'Lichtblitz des Lebens' and 'Donner
der Herzschlag'. Does not this explanation show how
well the text could be used in the above-mentioned order.
And so it is musically too. And yet it is different every-
time".*

---

* The quotations here are from Hildegard Jone's text. As may
be seen from p. 150, Webern eventually decided to put the Chariten
movement last, beginning with the "Lichtblitz des Lebens" and
putting the "Kleiner Fluegel" movement second.

The first public performance of Webern's first cantata took place at the I.S.C.M. festival in London in 1946.

31. *Orchestral Variations, Op. 30.* Composed in 1941,
first performance by Dr. Hermann Scherchen on 3rd
March, 1943 in Winterthur in Webern's presence. It was
his last journey abroad.

Webern wrote in a letter to Dr. Willi Reich on 3rd
March, 1941 about the variations: "... The piece lasts
about a quarter of on hour*, most of the way very fast in
tempo, but in part with the effect of a sostenuto. It should
– and I've kept to it – amount in form to a sort of Overture, but on the basis of variations. The title is: Variations
for Orchestra (op. 30). The instrumentation is kept small:
flute, oboe, clarinet, bass clarinet, horn, trumpet, tuba,
celeste, harp, timpani, strings (with double bass). It again
presents a synthesis: in form, 'horizontal', otherwise a
'vertical' presentation. Basically, my Overture is an
adagio form, but the reprise of the main theme appears
in the form of a development passage; so it contains this
element too. The 'Prometheus' by Beethoven and the
'Tragic' by Brahms are also overtures in adagio forms and
not in the form of a sonata movement."

* in fact about 8 minutes.

And again he wrote to Dr. Willi Reich on 3rd May, 1941 ". . . I should much like to explain the piece to you on the basis of the full score. But some important points in brief: the theme of the variations extends to the first double bar; it is periodic in form, but has an 'introductory' character. It is succeeded by six variations (each until the next double bar). In the first, the main theme of the Overture (in andante form) is completely stated, the second is the transition, the third the "second theme", the fourth the reprise of the main theme – it is an andante form – but in the form of a development section: the fifth, repeating the introduction and transition, leads to the coda, which is the sixth variation. Everything that occurs in the piece comes from the two phrases in the first and second bars (double bass and oboe). But it is further reduced since the second phrase (oboe) is in itself a palindrome. The second two notes are the retrograde of the first two, but rhythmically augmented. They are succeeded in the trombone by the first phrase (double bass) but in diminution. And in the retrograde of its motifs and intervals. This is the way in which my row is built, it uses these four notes three times.

"But the motivic sequence follows this cancrizan form, with, however, the use of augmentations and diminutions. These two kinds of alteration lead almost exclusively to the ideas of each variation, i.e. motivic alterations take place if at all only within these limits. But as a result of every possible shifting of the centre of gravity within the two phrases something new in rhythm, character, etc. is brought out. Compare the first repetition of the first phrase (trombone) with its first form (double bass). And so it goes through the whole piece which in its first twelve notes, i.e. in the row, contains the whole content in embryo form. It is pre-composed!!!"

In his letter to Hildegard Jone of 20th May, 1941 Webern provided a further interpretation of the score of his orchestral variations. To demonstrate his method of work, his precision and sense of responsibility, and his ability to discuss his work with someone really interested in it, an excerpt from the letter is reproduced here. "You want to know more about my recent work. How dear your question is to me! Imagine: here are six notes in a phrase determined in sequence and their rhythm, and what happens afterwards (in a piece lasting about twenty minutes)* is nothing but this phrase repeated. Naturally, in continuing 'metamorphosis' (musically this process is termed variation), but it is the same repeated phrase. This phrase first provides the 'theme' and then is followed by six variations on this theme. But the 'theme', as stated, is nothing but variations (metamorphoses of this phrase). As a *unit* it is again the starting point for new variations. But this theme with its six variations eventually results *formally* in a structure that can be compared to an 'adagio' form; but in *content* and in character this is not so – only in its form. Think of a classical 'overture'. So, even if I have called the piece 'Variations', they yet form a new unity (in the sene of a different form). A given number of metamorphoses of the first phrase produce the 'theme'. This, as a new unity again undergoes a given

* see note p. 152.

number of metamorphoses; in turn these are fused into a
new unity and provide the form of the whole. i.e. more or
less *the shape of the whole piece.* Perhaps all this will
tell you something?"

Op.30

32. *Second Cantata, Op.31, on a text by Hildegard Jone.*

The second cantata, the last completed work by
Webern, was begun in 1941 and completed in 1943. The
work is for soprano solo, bass solo, mixed chorus and
orchestra (small soloistic instrumentation: piccolo, flute,
oboe, cor anglais, clarinet, bass clarinet, alto-saxophone
in E flat, bassoon, horn, trumpet, trombone, tuba, bells,
glockenspiel, celeste, harp, strings); it is written in six
parts and in length it surpasses the first cantata (the whole
work lasts sixteen minutes):*

1. Bass solo with orchestra "Schweigt auch die
   Welt . . ." (Sehr lebhaft, in the form of an introductory recitative, 41 bars).
2. Bass solo with orchestra "Sehr tief verhalten . . ."
   (Sehr verhalten, bass aria, 17 bars).
3. Soprano solo, choir and orchestra "Schöpfer aus
   Brunnen des Himmels . . ." (Sehr bewegt, 59 bars).

* This is the timing given in the score. In actual performance,
however, the cantata lasts about 10½ mins.

4. Soprano solo with orchestra "Leichteste Bürde der
   Bäume ..." (Sehr lebhaft, 23 bars).

5. Soprano solo, violin solo, choir, orchestra "Freund-
   selig ist das Wort ..." (Sehr mässig, 60 bars).

6. Choir   and   orchestra   "Gelockert   aus   dem
   Schosse ..." (Sehr fliessend, double canon, 4 stan-
   zas).

While working on this composition – a work that in
some ways represents the final distillation of Webern's
specific last style – the composer repeatedly wrote to
Hildegard Jone, as well as to Dr. Willi Reich, about his
work; and this helps us towards a better understanding of
the composition. First Webern appears to have composed the complicated double canon which eventually
formed the third movement of the new cantata. He wrote
to Dr. Reich on 23rd August, 1941: "... I was totally
absorbed by my work (second cantata, op. 31) and
still am. The first movement of this new choral work
with soloists and orchestra – it will probably go beyond
the scope of a cantata – that at least is my plan – this
first movement is finished and already fully scored.
I should like at once to tell you something about it:
in form it is an introduction, a recitative, but basically
it is built on a structure never perhaps before imagined
by a "Netherlander"*. Perhaps it was the most difficult
task (in this respect) which I have ever had to undertake.
The basis is a canon in four parts of the most complicated

---

* i.e. one of the Flemish composers of the 16th century who used
complicated contrapuntal structures.

kind. Its execution (at least I believe so) was possible only
on the basis of the serial law, which here is quite particularly in evidence; indeed, its idea has here become
perhaps fully expressed for the first time. I read in
Plato that 'Nomos' (law) was identical with 'tune' (melody). Now the melody which the soprano solo sings in
my piece as an introduction (recitative), this may be the
law (nomos) for all that follows. In the sense of Goethe's
'primeval plant':" with this model and its key it will
be possible to invent an infinite number of plants . . . the
same law is applicable to all else that is living. – *Is this
not basically the essence of our serial law?*"

On 21st July, 1942, Webern again discussed the second
cantata, writing to Reich: "About my work I can report
that I have advanced a good long way. I was busy with
it in recent weeks: another piece of the planned 'oratorio'
is completely scored. It is an aria for soprano with chorus
and orchestra. One voice gives the law – in this case
it is the soprano solo – i. e. the 'melody' . . . That was the
way with the music of the masters. God only knows
whether I can achieve it as they did, but a least I am
aware of what it's all about. In my case, nothing takes
place that is not pre-determined by the 'melody'. It is the
'law' therefore truly the 'nomos'. But pre-determined
on the basis of a canon! Naturally, the 'row' represents a
law in itself: but it need not necessarily be the 'melody'
too. But since in my case it is in fact so, the 'row' now
assumes a special importance, so to speak on a higher
level, something perhaps like the chorale melodies in
Bach's arrangements. In general, the foundations of our

technique are there, but I believe that I am returning to them in a special way . . ."

On 4th September, 1942, the composer wrote further about his cantata, especially about the chorus which ends the work ("Gelockert aus dem Schosse . . .") ". . . In the meantime I have again completed a new piece – it is meant to form the first part of the planned 'oratorio' together with the earlier ones. It is for chorus and orchestra, so to speak a 'chorale'. But now again its inter-relations; the second part (alto) sings the retrograde of the first (tenor); the third (soprano) has the inversion of the second, and the fourth (bass) is the inversion of the first, and in addition the retrograde of the third! Thus a double interlinking of parts one and four, as well as of two and three (inversion relation) and again one and two as well as three and four (retrograde). I think that you will be surprised at the score. Long note values, but very flowing tempo."

On the 6th August, 1943, in a letter to Willi Reich, Webern again mentioned a part of the second cantata, which in its final form became No. 2, an aria for bass. Here is Webern's own commentary on it:

". . .I have hardly stopped working. Again a piece has been completed within the framework of the plan of which I have repeatedly spoken: a bass aria. This has become even stricter and, as a result, freer. That means to say, I am moving on the basis of a 'perpetual double canon in inversion' in complete freedom. Through variations, diminutions, etc. – something like Bach does with his theme in the 'Art of the Fugue'. But in its form the aria is in three sections with a theme of approximately thirty-two bars in periodic form; thus again, the closest inter-linking of the two forms of presentation. In character, a kind of hymn: "Die Stille um den Bienenkorb in der Heimat" ...

A letter to Reich of 22nd February, 1944, again reminisces about the second cantata, by then long completed, but as a result of the war not yet printed. From it Webern makes it clear that the work on the second cantata was only conditionally completed. He says:

"... As far as my work is concerned; having started on a 7th piece it became clear to me – what I had already sensed earlier – that *musically* I had reached an end with the completed six pieces, whether as a part of a larger work, or as a work in itself. I decided on the latter course, i.e. with a few changes I grouped these six movements together in one cantata: cantata No. 2 for soprano and bass soli, chorus and orchestra. Duration – half an hour ..."[*]

The second cantata had its first performance at the I.S.C.M. Festival in Brussels in 1950. Conductor, Herbert Haefner: soprano, Ilona Steingruber: bass, Otto Wiener.

Op.31

[*] see note p. 155.

ARNOLD SCHOENBERG
AS TEACHER

By Dr. Anton von Webern

The best reply to every malicious, jealous attack and calumny by reactionary minds against Schoenberg as a teacher is offered by his own essay, "Problems of Art Teaching" (published in "Musikalisches Taschenbuch", 11th edition 1911; Stern and Steiner.)

Never have words more penetrating or more truthful been said on this subject.

Every one of his pupils can himself experience what Schoenberg expresses in it. It is believed that Schoenberg teaches his own style and compels his pupils to adapt themselves to it. This is totally false.

Schoenberg teaches no style whatsoever; he advocates neither old nor new means of artistic expression. He says: "What sense is there in teaching the mastery of everyday cases? The pupil would learn to use something which he should not be using if he wants to be an artist. But the most important thing cannot be communicated: the courage and the strength of his attitude, so that everything he looks at becomes extraordinary as a result of the way he looks at it".

This "most important thing" is just what Schoenberg's pupils receive.

Schoenberg demands above all that his pupils should not simply fill in notes according to a school formula for their lessons, but that their work should spring from a need to express themselves.

That means that they do in fact create immediately even in the most elementary of musical constructions. Schoenberg's explanations to his pupils as a result of their works come organically from the works: there is no question of outside precepts.

Thus Schoenberg in fact teaches through creation.

With much energy he pursues every trace of the personality of his pupils, attempts to deepen it, to help them to express themselves, in short, to provide the pupil with "courage and strength", so that "everything he looks at becomes extraordinary as a result of the way he looks at it."

This is an education that teaches one to find the real truth in oneself.

Besides the purely musical it encompasses all other areas of human existence.

Yes, truly with Schoenberg one learns more than the rules of art. Those whose heart is open will be shown the path of good.

But how to explain that every one of his pupils who now works independently composes in a manner which is in style close to Schoenberg's? Certainly this is the main reason for the misunderstanding mentioned above concerning Schoenberg's teaching. No explanation for it can

be given. With this question we touch on the secret of
artistic creation in general.

Who can explain that?

There can be no question of a purely superficial adoption of these artistic means.

What then is it?

It is commanded by a need whose cause we do not know
but in which we must believe.

YOUTHFUL POEMS
Anton von Webern
(Probably 1901–2)

1. *Waldweg*	*Forest Path*
Auf grünem Moos mein Tritt	On green moss my step . . .
Der Waldbäume und Eriken Duft	The forest trees and heather
Wogt weich um meine Glieder	Wave softly round my limbs
Die Sonne ist schon ver- sunken	The sun has set already
Ihr letztes Rot	Its last red glow
Leuchtet	Shines
Durch die dunklen Stamme	Through the dark trunks
Die wie im Traume ihre Wipfel wiegen	Which cradle the tree-tops as in a dream
. . . .	. . . .
Meine Seele ist ruhig	My soul is at peace.

---

2. *Sonnenaufgang*	*Sunrise*
Herrlich strahlt sie empor,	Nobly he blazes on high,
Die Siegerin,	The conqueror
Wie unter Jauchzen	As with the shouts
Von Millionen Stimmen.	Of a million voices

Ha, nun taucht sie in leuchtende Flut	Ha, now he plunges in the shining flood
Die Welt. –	The world –
Gewichen das Dunkel	Darkness has yielded
Licht, allüberall Licht!	Light, everywhere light!

---

3. *Frauenschönheit*	*Woman's Beauty*
Wie weicher Mondesglanz	Like a soft moonbeam
Auf duftenden Rosen	On scented roses
Wie ein träumender Brunnen	Like a dreaming spring
Unter einer Trauerweide	Under a weeping willow
In heller Sommernacht	On a clear summer night
Wie die Frühlingssonne	Like the spring sun
Am strahlenden Morgen	On a shining morning
Wie ein Duft von blauen Veilchen	Like a scent of blue violets
Die im Frühling träumen …	Dreaming in spring …
Ach, wie das unsagbare Wehen	Ah, like the marvellous waves
Von weichen Palmenduften	Of soft palm breezes
So, so bist du, Frauenschönheit!	So art thou, beauty of woman!

---

4. *An den Preglhof*	*To the Preglhof*
Irgendwo,	Somewhere,
Ganz fern	Far away
Liegt ein liebes, liebes Haus	Lies a dear, dear house
Hohe, schlanke Pappeln	Tall, slim poplars
Umsäumen es	Enclose it.

So lieblich schaut es in die Welt,	So lovely it seems in the world,
Weich weht der Wind dort	Soft blows the wind there
Dort ist Ruhe,	There is rest,
Tiefer Friede herrscht	Deep peace rules there
Mein Herz sehnt sich dort- hin	My heart longs to go there
Über die Berge hin, bis zu	Over the mountains to
Jenen Pappeln, jenen hohen, schlanken	Those poplars, those tall slim poplars
Die das liebe Haus um- säumen	Which enclose the dear house,
. . . Irgendwo,	. . .Somewhere
Ganz fern . . .	Far away . . .

ANTON WEBERN

An article by Dr. Theodor Wiesengrund-Adorno

(from "Anbruch", Viennese Musical Journal, 1926, Volume 6, 8th year, on the occasion of the perform-ance of the 5 Orchestral pieces op. 10, in Zürich).

The difficulty and exclusivity of Webern's works stem from the fact of the relation between prescribed form and personal freedom having been broken, since we ac-cord the right to the individual to choose his forms; while musical comprehension is normally supplemented by a tension existing between the community and the individ-ual. This tension reaches from the community to the indi-vidual and lays the community open to the explosive ideas of the individual.

In Webern's case the will of the individual has demol-ished the commonly accepted forms once and for all. The traditional prescribed forms yield to an attack of the sub-jective-expressive force. Their reality has long been demol-ished, and their semblance proved insufficient to hold the mind which in its loneliness concentrates on truth. Like almost no other, Webern's music corresponds to the de-mands of expressionism. Without permitting the question of its valid objectivity, it is satisfied with the pure presen-tation of the subjective which cannot be divorced from the

musical material. Its objectivity is realised in the form of
a true, exact and uncompromising self-determination of
the material. Within such limitations it appears to have
no past; according to this concept absolute lyricism is
only comprehensible to itself. If Webern's expressionistic
miniatures need subtle interpretation to be understood,
they also flee from it. "Whatever one says, no words can
do justice to this music", Webern wrote of Schoenberg's
"Little Piano Pieces" (op. 19), which were the nearest
to his own music. Recourse to any existing forms prove
impossible from the start since Webern's music denies
them. The area of tension that can be interpreted in it
shrinks to nothing; the radical unity of its intention and
appearance forbids words.

Especially this, and the demand the music makes to be
free of history, in forbidding every contemporary tendency in its expression, links it with history. Its extreme
individualism is the completion of the romantic. The
stress is on the very point which marks the change. It is
this pupilhood which marked Webern's music, earning
it the reproof of being totally dependent. If his
works are still today undervalued, then it is partly the
fault of the view that this suspect individualist had developed no individuality of his own, borrowing instead from
the master. This view does Webern an injustice. Not to
mention the fact that the interval between the first works
of Schoenberg that had emancipated themselves from
tonality was considerably shorter than that between
Debussy's and Ravel's first stylistically mature works –
and in spite of similarities there is no question there of

dependence – this view overlooks the specific structure
of those very compositions of Schoenberg which provided
the decisive impetus for Webern. Their sign is the dis-
appearance of the prescribed form; and Schoenberg's
technique, as for example in the third piano piece of op.
11, is only characterised in that it controls the immanent
mood of the image in relation to the subjective intention.
If Webern's technique and criticisms accepted the
Schoenberg of the Georgelieder and the first piano pieces,
he followed, irrespective of the identity of the means, in
the first place a historic line which Schoenberg represented, rather than losing himself in Schoenberg. In both
the means, agreeing polemically, result positively in a
different expression. While those works of Schoenberg's
lead through a heightened romantic expressive music and
tectonic objectivity towards a new personal freedom, and
from there to constructions which stimulate the imagination, but, bordering on the anarchic, foreshadow principles
of novel construction, Webern's absolute lyricism, without
aim in itself and thus throughout complete in itself.

After all this it might be assumed that Webern's music
is neither historically linked nor shows any development.
But its origin is truly dialectic and it contains enough
dialectical anti-theses to develop within the small framework it set itself. Also, it is related, as late romanticism,
to psychology, with its blind infinity which does not allow
it to stand still. The early works clearly show its dialectic
origins. In the same way as Alban Berg, the symphonic
composer to whom Schoenberg's chamber symphony
pointed the way, wrote expressionistic miniatures in

Webern's sense before he built his orchestral works, so
Webern, the lyrical poet, proved himself in the strictest
forms until he felt capable of understanding himself –
"without regrets", as Schoenberg put it. His op. 1 is a passacaglia; his op. 2 a double canon. The experimental
harmonic style – psychologically heightened and prepared to develop by the middle Schoenberg period – was
compelled to keep within a self-imposed pattern. The
works that follow, two sets of songs on poems by Stefan
George, attenuate the idea of absolute lyricism to break-
ing point. Almost completely atonal, they already possess
the melodic metric freedom of the later works and the
natural immediacy of a deeply felt emotion.

But motivically they are still tied, and the piano
writing is influenced by the easy figuration and the chor-
dal richness of the instrument. The Five Movements for
String Quartet op. 5, of which the first reproduces in
exemplary form the sonata type movement in 55 bars,
still use motifs. But the manner is thoroughly rationalised,
the thematic units employed are small in a way which
foreshadows the mature Webern in its form. In the brevity of the second, fourth and fifth movements an expressionistic miniature is crystallised. It also manifests itself in
the Four Pieces for Violin and Piano, op. 4 (1910), the Six
Bagatelles for String Quartet, op. 9 (1913), the Five Orchestral Pieces, op. 10 (1913) and the Three Small Pieces
for Cello and Piano, op. 11 (1914). The works belonging
to this group are thought through to their logical end as
few others are: their continuation would have been a sigh
alone. The melodic line is divided into freely changing

particles, which are eventually reduced to a single note. The arrangement of the whole, utterly brief, is void of symmetry. The counterpoint economically points the separate lines against each other; it no longer recognises linear writing. The sound is separated from the individual nature of the instruments, seeking to employ to the full their most remote potentialities. Everything that has gone before in music is extinguished. It obeys the spirit and the spirit shines through it. Webern realised the concept of "melody of tone colour". After this, during the war, he slightly changed. The Lieder op. 12 possess the economy of the earlier compositions, but in essence are much simpler, returning to the melodic line. The first verse of the first song is even an eight-bar period with a caesura in the fourth bar. The most recently published works by Webern (1928), the Chamber Songs after Trakl op. 14, and the Sacred Songs op. 15, with their carefully selected chamber orchestration, pursue their lyrical aim with a new, tender polyphony in broken curves. They show distantly an echo of the storm which Schoenberg raised against the closed doors of musical objectivity. It is a lonely intellect which trembles yet remains firm; there was nothing else left to it.

That Webern should have set the poet Trakl should be understood symbolically. Both are at home in a lonely sphere. The work of both grows out of a detached inwardnes; the work of both sounds the needs of a melancholy mind. Both demonstrate the loneliness of God's creature. They speak of him but the echo fades.

ANTON WEBERN'S
FIFTIETH BIRTHDAY
An article by Dr. Heinrich Jalovec
(From Musical section of "Anbruch",
Vienna November/December, 1933.)

...Webern's creative impulse springs from his nature, a vision of things which cannot be expressed other than musically. Visions of an individual universe heard only through unprecedented sounds and a deep dislike of everything "traditional" determined his early beginnings. If Schoenberg created a new musical alphabet on the basis of the traditional, then Webern speaks with this alphabet in a highly personal manner.

The basis of his whole personality rests on creation, human and divine. His manner as a conductor is not demanding but passionately devoted, like that of a gardener with his flowers. Yet he does not seek nature in a primitivity which denies tradition, but through the greatest possible freeing of the musical material – a freeing of the hard surface contours not known to nature, neither the outer nor the inner, neither the world of blossom and scents nor that of the human heart and spiritual forms. He does not paint an impressionistic picture with tiny mosaic-like, repeated motifs. But his works have melody. They are not served as an appetising dish to a sensual

ear, nor are they kept in a formal cast which, detached
from the rich structure of the whole, could live by itself.
His music is something almost intangible, made up of
sounds, intervals, floating rhythms and widely ramified
melodic elements; it just suffices to express an incredibly tender and intense sentiment.

Yet the documents of this secret but vigorous world are
not amorphous; they are governed by proportion and
organic growth. Throughout these free images, with their
floating rhythms, runs a thread, thin yet as firm as any
tangible superficial pattern. It is even more forceful,
since the tension bridging this "filigree-like" work accords with the human tension that is the motive force of
these works. Through the identification of artist and
work, feeling and form, all become "absolute" music with
an immediacy rare today. But since it is beyond all "pre-
mises" it is easily misunderstood, especially by musicians.

This directness essentially leads to a unique sensitivity
for anything that is too noisy, heavy, tangible or simply
too much; a refusal to be loquacious which on occasions
goes so far that a piece consists of just one theme, one
period.

All this should not be misunderstood: one should not
imagine that Webern instinctively improvises. The
greatest care and conscientiousness are at work here, permitting nothing by chance, and no rest until each work
bears the proportions and the naturalness of a piece of
nature . . .

ANTON WEBERN
By Dr. Hans Mersmann
(from Bueckens Handbooks, Volume "New Music"
page 144.)

... the two most sharply outlined personalities whose
music points in this direction (the twelve-note music of
the "New Vienna School" around Schoenberg) are Anton
Webern and Alban Berg. Both demonstrate the different
possibilities of a development starting at this point. With
alarming clarity Webern shows the way of a musician
who has developed beyond Schoenberg, and who has cast
away all those inhibitions which still affect Schoenberg's
works. On his side Alban Berg is more positive, more
active; he possess abilities that creatively overcome the
process of decomposition threatening Webern.

Webern's works demonstrate the great danger result-
ing from Schoenberg's development. He, too, writes
"pieces" for violin and piano, for string quartet or for
orchestra. While this form means the highest degree of
concentration for Schoenberg, filled with a tense activity,
the same process takes Webern off the rails. Development, form, the will to build has long vanished from
his music; it can no longer form, hardly breathe. I reproduce here the fourth of his "Five Pieces for Orchestra,
op. 10". The six bars are one "piece". Here and there a

sparse, fine, dismembered sound, a few figures in the mandoline, trumpet and violin, torn, isolated single notes, that is all. The score, for eleven instruments, makes an ironic impression. The dynamics descend from piano to a triple pianissimo. Should one meet with this music without realising from which position and circle it had grown, one would regard it as the work of a practical joker, or a junior pupil in composition making fun of modern music. Nothing objectively differentiates this music from it, but the name of its composer. This is the end of a path. We are faced with the end of music, the final point reached simultaneously by the other arts; with the painter being content to indicate a few strokes, or to oppose two simple colours; with sculpture hardening into stereometric figures; with drama consisting of nothing but a few disconnected words. Kurt Schwitters wrote a "drama" in which the actors only speak in vowel sounds. Again the ghost of dadaism appears. We are at an end.

If anywhere, it becomes clear here that this most recent development is nothing but the last continuation of the impressionistic process of decay of all coherence. And how far it is removed from building and form. Webern's vocal music pursues the same path. The destruction of the word-melody through over-stressing of the large intervals and the unreality of the time-values – these two roots of Schoenberg's development return here also.

Where they lead Webern is shown by the following example (quotation of the melodic line of the first bars of "Steht auf, ihr lieben Kinderlein" from the "Geistliche Lieder" op. 15) with an exaggerated sharpness through its opposition to the text. What can be understood as sublime reflection and intellectual complexity in Stefan George, is clearly shown here in all its inner contradictions with a sharp force in the clear light of dawn.

SPEECH BY DR. DAVID JOSEF BACH

On the fiftieth birthday of Anton Webern
on December, 1933
in the Small Hall of the Vienna Musikverein.

Ladies and Gentlemen,
Dear Friend Webern,

Fifty years of a life are not by themselves a complete whole. They are literally a half century and they belong to the century from which they spring and out of which they lead. The artist belongs to his time – and he leads the time. That is true also of the *physical* concept of time, whose admitted relativity has been the most decisive event of scientific thought of the past half century; even this physical time is a part of the artist and is carried by him. But he is privileged: his time is not perhaps better than another. But the hour which he strikes is the time that can be heard. It is a time that defines and can be defined within the stream of a development in which we at will select definable points.

The will alone that wants to orient itself is not without laws and meets nature within the framework of laws. The artist whose fate it is to be nature itself and to create anew obeys such laws. Or, expressed spiritually, the artist is fated so consciously to insist on the individual and to

176

render it valid that through it he creates a new wider consciousness.

The personal development of a master such as Anton Webern, nourished by multiple sources from the past and the present, determined by personal rules within and around him (since the relations between one individual and others, including the general community, are as much free choice as predetermined fate); this development can perhaps best be understood as a projection of the general new world in an individual form. This is not to diminish it. Since, to speak with the philosophers, individual existence is the realised ideal of God. Further, Leibniz once wrote: "Individuality is the lawful change of the existing condition. . . . The law of change results in the individuality of the each substance". For none is this more valid than for the musician. But music has not stood still at these reflections of Leibniz, which have influenced thought for centuries. Certainly, it may be interpreted as the realisation of a pre-stabilised harmony, alone capable of keeping in being the world of the monads, of the individual existence. This thought does not spring from a play on the word "harmony". But music is an exceptionally good means of providing the monads with a consciousness of their own within the general consciousness; and it is this which is in the general sense termed harmony. Within this eternal task, music moves; in Anton Webern we greet the creator of new forms of this idea. New times have new music, as it creates a new world with which music is philosophically and physically linked. Do not the twelve notes, and the

absence of a relation to a preferred tonic, do they not
correspond to the removal of the chosen, strict system of
co–ordination in the physical world? The principles
governing the world have become relative, like those of
music, without losing in force or binding strength. On
the contrary. The equal relations – always new – between
the twelve notes create just the link necessary for the individual to reach the most complete freedom, i.e. the
unfolding of the highest laws.

The new co-ordinate of time, added to the other
given determinants, plays a decisive role in the case
of the composer Anton Webern. He moves with the
musical event, which means life to him; and in so doing
the measure, the development and the tempo of his
music is determined in each instance. Those outside –
and for long enough they were the listeners – consider the
tempo too fast, the measure too brief. It is only when we
experience it ourselves that, together with the composer,
we join the trend of events and recognise the natural
lawful course.

Twenty-five years ago, it would have been possible
to speak here and there, borrowing from other arts, of
"impressionism". The famous "As I see it" of Peter
Altenberg can be countered by an "As I hear it" of Anton
Webern. But because the world was capable of understanding that music only after 20 or 30 years it does not
mean that the music is tied to a contemporary style or
a fashion. Each brief piece of Webern's says what
it has to say, and says it completely. Twenty years ago,
when music had turned towards a new basis, but had

not yet completed the change, when music like science moved on more through what it disregarded than what it retained, did we not speculate in philosophical or mathematical terms, ending with the warning "Is this the end of the song?" Did we not prove mathematically that the number of possible melodic combinations was not only limited but also nearly exhausted? The end of the song was simultaneously the end of a mechanistic view of the world. Today we know that the world is finite but unlimited, and so music is unlimited in its melodic possibilities.

Anton Webern showed new possibilities of this kind. Whoever studies his works carefully knows that Webern found new means to get the attention of the listener. But, as Ernst Mach once said, the art of the composer requires the art of the listener, which is not a thing for everyone. Really not? Then we face a new task for music and at the same time a new and major achievement of the musician Webern. If he as a composer was able within the limits of music to realise the new physical world image, then as a conductor he succeeded in bringing about a general consciousness of works of art, a real linking of a community that feels itself *as one* with the artist and his work. Once it was thought that, to lay stress on the particular artistic merits of music, music need meet no practical requirements. How? Does the community feeling of music meet no practical needs? Music as the realisation of an idea, as the true reality of scientific formulae also gaining life through it and becoming the general content of consciousness – does this meet no practical need? The conductor Webern leads music as an art form back to life; he penetrates the dividing wall separating each individual work of art from general experience; and he realises the idea of the work of art; he renders it true.

This is an *affirmation of life itself,* which is characteristic of Webern the artist, the composer and the conductor. His art is no refuge from life, however much envy, and that persecution to which every artist is exposed, appear to represent it as such. In truth, it is a proud path into life itself . . . To be able to follow him on this path, that is at one and the same time a sense of gratitude and happiness for us. As Nietzsche sang about the journey to new oceans –

> "That is where I will go – and I believe
> in myself and in my grasp"

and so we speak with our love and with our best wishes:

> "That is where you will go – and you believe
> in yourself and in your grasp".

BIBLIOGRAPHY
and
DISCOGRAPHY

Innumerable articles have been written about Webern, and a large bibliography of these is given in Kontrapunkte Vol. 5, Anton Webern, by Walter Kolneder, published by P. J. Tonger, 1961. (English translation in preparation). Books concerning Webern in English are few: the most important is the recently published "The Path to the New Music", (Universal Edition and Theodore Presser Co.), which is a transcript of Webern's lectures given in Vienna in 1932–3; Vol. 2 of Die Reihe is a symposium on Webern in English (also Universal Edition), and the same publishers have brought out (in German) Webern's letters to Hildegard Jone and Josef Humplik. A further symposium, Anton Webern, Weg und Gestalt (in German), edited by Willi Reich, is published by Die Arche, Zurich, and Dr. Hans Moldenhauer's "The Death of Anton Webern" (Vision Press and Philosophical Library) gives a fully documented account of his tragic end. Further useful sources are René Leibowitz' books "Schoenberg and his School" (Hinrichsen) and "Introduction à la Musique de Douze Sons" (L'Arche, Paris).

Webern's complete works, including the early piano quintet and the orchestration of the 6-part Ricercare from Bach's "Musical Offering", have been recorded under the direction of Robert Craft for Philips (U. S. Columbia). Pierre Boulez has recorded the two Cantatas for French Vega, and Philips (U. S. Columbia) also issue the Five Movements, Op. 5, by the Juilliard Quartet and the same work in the version for string orchestra, again conducted by Robert Craft.

INDEX OF NAMES